MARTIN PURYEAR

MARTIN PURYEAR

BY NEAL BENEZRA

WITH AN ESSAY BY ROBERT STORR

THAMES AND HUDSON
THE ART INSTITUTE OF CHICAGO

Martin Puryear was prepared on the occasion of the exhibition of the same title, organized by The Art Institute of Chicago in 1991. It was made possible in part by a grant from the Lannan Foundation. Additional support for this catalogue and the exhibition it accompanied was received from the National Endowment for the Arts, a Federal agency.

Copublished by The Art Institute of Chicago and Thames and Hudson. First published in the United States of America in 1991 by Thames and Hudson Inc., 500 Fifth Avenue, New York, New York 10110 Reprinted in paperback 1993

The Art Institute of Chicago
Executive Director of Publications: Susan F. Rossen
Associate Director of Publications: Robert V. Sharp
Production Manager: Katherine Houck Fredrickson

Edited by Terry Ann R. Neff and Robert V. Sharp
Designed by Alex Castro, Baltimore, Maryland
Typeset in Gill Sans Light by Paul Baker Typography, Inc., Evanston, Illinois
Printed and bound by Dai Nippon Printing Co., Ltd., Tokyo, Japan

Library of Congress Catalog Card Number 91-65308

Photography Credits
Amherst, Massachusetts, University of Massachusetts Gallery, Fred Moore: p. 142; Boston, The Museum of Fine Arts: figs. 11, 12; Boston, Frederick R. Wulsin: fig. 10; Chicago, The Art Institute of Chicago, Thomas Cinoman: cat. nos. 2, 4, 17, 38; Carl Basner: figs. 1-5, 9, 19, 20; Chicago, Chicago Photographic Co., Kenneth C. Burkhart: opening illustration; Russell B. Phillips: fig. 21; Chicago, Chicago Tribune Co., Ron Bailey: p. 138; Chicago, Museum of Contemporary Art, Tom Van Eynde: fig. 14; Chicago, Michael Tropea: cover, cat. nos. 1, 6, 8, 12, 13, 18, 24, 27, 31, 34, 35, 40, fig. 35, p. 151; Chicago, Donald Young Gallery: cat. nos. 33, 36, 37, figs. 29, 36, p. 12; Dallas, The Dallas Museum of Art: cat. no. 30; Detroit, Dirk Bakker: figs. 23, 24; La Jolla, California, La Jolla Museum of Contemporary Art: frontispiece; Lewiston, New York, Artpark, Andrew L. Strout: figs. 15, 16; Los Angeles, The Museum of Contemporary Art, Gene Ogami: fig. 13; Los Angeles, Douglas Parker: cat. nos. 14, 20-23, 39, figs. 30, 32, 34, p. 153; Milwaukee, The Milwaukee Art Museum, Dedra Walls: p. 149; Minneapolis, The Walker Art Center, Glen Halvorson: cat. no. 28, figs. 28, 31; Munich, Bernd Klüser Gallery, Philipp Schönborn: fig. 37; New York, The American Museum of Natural History: fig. 26; New York, Rudolph Burckhardt: fig. 6; New York, Sheldan Collins: cat. no. 29; New York, The Museum of Modern Art: cat. no. 19; New York, The Solomon R. Guggenheim Museum: cat. no. 3; David Heald: fig. 33; Robert E. Mates: p. 146; New York, Sarah Wells: cat. nos. 5, 9, 11, 16, figs. 17, 27, pp. 9, 126, 140, 144, 154; New York, Whitney Museum of American Art, Geoffrey Clements: cat. no. 26; Omaha, The Joslyn Art Museum: cat. no. 7; Philadelphia, Philadelphia Museum of Art: cat. no. 25; San Antonio, Roger Fry: cat. no. 15; Seattle, Art on File: figs. 18, 25; University Park, Illinois, Governors State University, Nathan Manilow Sculpture Park, Richard Burd: fig. 22; Washington, D.C., The Corcoran Gallery of Art: fig. 8; Washington, D.C., Thore Crespi, courtesy of U.S. Information Agency: figs. 38, 39; Washington, D.C., Rick Gardner: cat. no. 10; Washington, D.C., Hirshhorn Museum and Sculpture Garden, Smithsonian Institution, Lee Stalsworth: cat. no. 32.

Opening illustration:
Martin Puryear constructing *Yurt* (for *Where the Heart Is [Sleeping Mews]*) at the Chicago Public Library Cultural Center, Chicago, 1987

Frontispiece:
Installation of the exhibition "Martin Puryear: Ten Year Survey," La Jolla Museum of Contemporary Art, La Jolla, California, 1984

CONTENTS

FOREWORD

Martin Puryear moved to Chicago in 1978, soon after a disastrous fire had destroyed his Brooklyn studio and most of his sculpture. He came to Chicago ostensibly to accept a teaching position at the University of Illinois, Chicago, but also to establish new roots after the trauma of the fire. Puryear's warmth and intelligence, as well as the growing quality of his work, quickly won him friends and admirers here. In 1980 he established an ongoing relationship with the Young Hoffman Gallery (and later the Donald Young Gallery), and in that same year he was awarded a solo exhibition at the Museum of Contemporary Art.

In 1982 Puryear was invited to participate in the "74th American Exhibition" at The Art Institute of Chicago. He exhibited two works, and when one, *Sanctuary*, was awarded the Mr. and Mrs. Frank G. Logan Prize, the Art Institute was able to acquire the sculpture for the permanent collection. In 1989 a second work, *Lever #1*, a haunting, monumental sculpture, was also purchased for the museum. Puryear was able to nurture his work and his career to maturity in Chicago, and because of the very personal nature of his relationship to this city, we at the Art Institute take great pride in organizing the most ambitious presentation of his work to date.

The quality of the institutions participating in this exhibition testifies to the level of Puryear's achievement. We are grateful to James T. Demetrion, Director, Hirshhorn Museum and Sculpture Garden, Washington, D.C.; Richard Koshalek, Director, The Museum of Contemporary Art, Los Angeles; and Anne d'Harnoncourt, Director, Philadelphia Museum of Art, for their commitment to and involvement in this project. Finally, we are deeply indebted to the Lannan Foundation for their early and enthusiastic support of this exhibition.

James N. Wood
Director

Martin Puryear, *Circumbent*, 1976
Ash
62 in. x 10 ft. 1 in. x 21 in.
Collection of the artist

ACKNOWLEDGMENTS

For a number of years the sculpture of Martin Puryear was a relatively well-kept secret. Working rather quietly and teaching in Chicago, Puryear produced only a modest number of sculptures annually. Although a remarkably high percentage of Puryear's works were entering museum collections, for the most part these sculptures were seen only individually, either in the context of permanent collections or in group exhibitions. The one touring exhibition of Puryear's work to date was organized by Hugh M. Davies for the University Gallery, University of Massachusetts, Amherst, in 1984.

In part, the modest pace of the development of Puryear's career has reflected the artist's own personality. Never a seeker of the limelight, Puryear relishes the opportunity to work in the studio, unburdened by the pressure that media and market attention can produce. This situation changed rather dramatically in 1988–89. During that two-year period, Puryear was awarded a grant from the John D. and Catherine T. MacArthur Foundation, he was selected to represent the United States in the twentieth São Paulo Bienal (where his exhibition of eight sculptures was awarded the grand prize), and The Art Institute of Chicago announced plans for the present exhibition of his work.

As detailed in James N. Wood's foreword, the Art Institute has a long-standing relationship with Puryear both as exhibitor and collector, and in many ways it was natural that we should produce this exhibition. I am grateful to Director James N. Wood; the late James W. Alsdorf, Chairman of the Committee on Exhibitions and the Committee on Twentieth-Century Painting and Sculpture; and Charles F. Stuckey, Curator, Department of Twentieth-Century Painting and Sculpture, for their wholehearted support of this project virtually from the moment I suggested it. The enthusiasm for Puryear's work in the American museum community is great, and the quality of the three museums participating in the tour testifies to the widespread admiration for the sculpture. I would like to add my thanks to James T. Demetrion, Ned Rifkin, and Amada Cruz, Hirshhorn Museum and Sculpture Garden, Washington, D.C.; Richard Koshalek, Mary Jane Jacob, Paul Schimmel, Sherri Geldin, Alma Ruiz, and Julie Lazar, The Museum of Contemporary Art, Los Angeles; and Anne d'Harnoncourt, Ann Temkin, and Suzanne F. Wells, Philadelphia Museum of Art.

A number of individuals at the Art Institute have been crucial to the realization of this exhibition. I am especially indebted to Dorothy Schroeder, Assistant Director for Exhibitions and Budget; Mary Solt, Executive Director of Museum Registration; William R. Leisher, Executive Director of Museum Conservation; Larry Ter Molen, Vice-President for Development and Public Affairs; and Mary Jane Keitel, Director of Foundation and Government Relations. Numerous other individuals have been exceptionally helpful, and I especially want to recognize Reynold Bailey, Eliza Hatch, Maureen Lasko, John Molini, Mary Mulhern, Emily Romero, and Jennifer Trezona for their efforts.

In the Twentieth-Century Department, I am particularly grateful to three individuals whose dedicated attention to detail was crucial to the realization of this project. Nancy Owen and Carole Tormollan served as research assistants, contributing to every aspect of this publication and co-authoring the documentation section. Eddi Wolk assisted me throughout the project and I am thankful for her devoted efforts. Courtney Donnell, Mary Murphy, Nicholas Barron, Heidi O'Neill, Neville Gay, and Kate Heston were always helpful and a pleasure to work with.

The catalogue has been produced by the Art Institute's Publications Department, under the direction of Susan F. Rossen. I am indebted to Robert V. Sharp, Associate Director of Publications, Production Manager Katherine Houck Fredrickson, and Terry Ann R. Neff, guest editor of this volume, as well as to Cris Ligenza. My thanks are due Robert Storr for his essay, Susan Dwyer of Thames and Hudson, and, for the elegant design of this publication, to Alex Castro, assisted by Susan Johnson of Chicago. We have rephotographed as many of Puryear's sculptures as time and budget would allow, and I am grateful to Sarah Wells, Michael Tropea, Douglas Parker, Nori Sato, and Glen Halvorson, as well as Thomas Cinoman of the Art Institute staff, for their fine work. At crucial junctures, James Ulak, Associate Curator of Japanese Art, and Ramona Austin, Assistant Curator of African Art, have contributed important ideas and information.

All of us have relied extensively on Martin Puryear's gallery representatives, who have given tirelessly of themselves and their archives. My efforts, in particular, have at times been excessive in obtaining information and loans, and I want to thank Donald Young, Margo Leavin, David and Renee McKee, and Nancy Drysdale for their patience and good spirit of cooperation. Their assistants — Barbara Mirecki of the Donald Young Gallery; Wendy Brandow, Kathryn Kanjo, and Lynn Sharpless of the Margo Leavin Gallery; and Howard Watler and Bruce Hackney of the David McKee Gallery — have provided invaluable assistance and we are very grateful.

Thanks are also due numerous other individuals who have lent their efforts to this project: Roger and Neil Barrett, Gwen Bits, Peter W. Boswell, Edward R. Broida, Trevor Fairbrother, John and Martha Gabbert, Michael Glass, Kathy Halbreich, Henri, Mary Jane Jacob, Kellie Jones, Marisa Keller, Elaine King, Gregory V. Knight, James Krenov, Rex Moser, Mark Ochmanek, Brenda Richardson, Nell Sonneman, Janet Stanley, John Vinci, and Colin Westerbeck. I would also like to thank Albert E. Elsen, whose enthusiasm for sculpture has long influenced my own, and Maria Makela, whose presence is implicit in each of the pages that follow.

The organization of this exhibition has coincided with a period of great change in Martin Puryear's life. Beyond the increased recognition of his work on a national and international level, Puryear recently retired from teaching in order to concentrate fully on his work in the studio and, along with the architect John Vinci, he recently designed a new house and studio in New York State. During this dynamic period, Puryear has been exceedingly generous and open with his time and attention, and he and his wife, Jeanne, have been very gracious hosts as well as becoming good friends. The most a curator can hope for in working with an artist is the opportunity to see art and the world through another set of eyes and to have his own world enriched in the process. I am grateful to Martin Puryear for providing me with just such an opportunity.

Neal Benezra
Curator
Department of Twentieth-Century Painting and Sculpture

"THE THING SHINES, NOT THE MAKER":
THE SCULPTURE OF MARTIN PURYEAR

By Neal Benezra

"Freedom" is a word that is now being used rather too carelessly, and Buddhists prefer the word muge…which refers to the absence of that impediment or restriction arising from relativity. It means the state of liberation from all duality, a state where there is nothing to restrict or be restricted. Beauty then ought to be understood as the beauty of liberation or freedom from impediment.

Martin Puryear, *Desire*, 1981
Pine, red cedar, poplar, and Sitka spruce
16 ft. x 16 ft. x 31 ft. 10 in.
Panza di Biumo Collection, Milan

These words are drawn from Soetsu Yanagi's *The Unknown Craftsman*, a well-known series of essays written on Eastern craft aesthetics by the acknowledged founder of the Japanese crafts movement.[1] Throughout these essays, Yanagi characterizes the aesthetic of Eastern craft as a reconciliation of opposites, or, perhaps more appropriately, the embrace of opposites. It is an aesthetic without "polarized concepts," in which notions of freedom are tied to an absence of impediments imposed from within by the artist or externally by one's context. The artist possesses a freedom that may be intuitive and inclusive, rather than proscriptive and bound by context, tradition, or practice. This is a truly expansive notion for it redefines beauty as based not in a specific set of idealized precepts, but rather as a "liberation from duality."

Martin Puryear has traveled in Japan and he is familiar with Eastern aesthetics; indeed, he knows Yanagi's essays very well. And yet, while Puryear would subscribe to these ideas of the freedom of the spirit, he does so not because he embraces Eastern thought exclusively; rather, these ideas confirm his interest in an enormous variety of approaches. His experience and understanding of the art, craft, and thought of numerous cultures on several continents has encouraged a pluralism of the creative spirit that is perhaps unparalleled in contemporary art. That is, while many contemporary sculptors have focused rather exclusively on specific problems of form or content, Puryear has consistently avoided the temptation to narrow his outlook. By exploring and embracing, rather than excluding and refining, Puryear has been able to create a body of work that is rich with the possibilities of the unseen.

Yanagi's thought is important for Puryear in another, perhaps more obvious, way. Throughout these essays, this advocate of craft espouses the value of the handmade; objects made with commitment, concentration, and sensitivity, and without the constraints of ego, in which, as Yanagi noted, "the thing shines, not the maker,"[2] may have a transforming power. This philosophy of craft constituted Puryear's starting point, and the manner in which he has transformed these ideas into a body of compelling and original handmade sculpture is the essence of his story.

Fig. 1
Martin Puryear, *Untitled*, 1965
Ink and wash on tan wove paper
11¹¹⁄₁₆ × 8¹¹⁄₁₆ in.
Collection of the artist

The oldest of seven children, Martin Puryear was born on May 23, 1941, in Washington, D.C. His father, Reginald, is a retired post-office supervisor; his mother, Martina, a retired public grade-school teacher. From his youth Puryear possessed an affinity for drawing and painting, but also for building useful objects. As Puryear would later recall, "If I became interested in archery, I made the bows and arrows; if I became interested in music, I made the guitar."[3] Puryear was also a serious reader, searching out information on things that fascinated him, and he read incessantly about topics ranging from Native Americans to ornithology and from archery to falconry. The study of nature and wildlife were Puryear's prevailing school-age interests; his youthful ambition was to be a wildlife illustrator, and his first attempts at making art were small drawings and paintings of specific birds and animals.[4] Forty years later Puryear can still identify the species he depicted, and clearly his youthful enthusiasm was as much ornithological and zoological as artistic. Falconry held a particular fascination and would become a lasting interest; although Puryear never practiced falconry, he collected books on the subject and made hoods for a hawk that he hoped to catch.

Following graduation from high school in 1958, Puryear entered Catholic University in Washington. His interest in natural phenomena led him first to the study of biology; he did not begin to study art seriously until his junior year. The influence of Color-Field painters such as Morris Louis, Helen Frankenthaler, Gene Davis, and Kenneth Noland predominated in Washington at this time, and Noland taught at Catholic University from 1951 to 1960. Although Noland's tenure at the school ended before Puryear entered the art program, the older artist did serve indirectly as an influence, for he was Puryear's first example of a working, professional artist.[5]

Although Puryear today remembers the art department at Catholic University as very conservative, at that time he was himself obsessed with traditional values in art, expressing his admiration for artists such as Pieter Brueghel and Andrew Wyeth, and dismissing abstraction as lacking in substance and meaning.[6] The young artist's attitude toward abstraction began to change during his undergraduate years. This was due in large measure to Nell Sonneman, Puryear's most important instructor at Catholic. Sonneman joined the faculty at Catholic University in 1959, following periods of study at the University of North Carolina, the Art Students' League, and New York State Ceramics College at Alfred University. An illustrator, ceramist, fiber artist, and painter, Sonneman taught courses in painting and the philosophy of art, the latter emphasizing art as an activity of the mind and spirit as well as the hand. Sonneman has outlined the ideas that underlay the philosophy course in which Puryear enrolled:

Art is a habit of the intellect, developed with practice over time, that empowers the artist
to make the work right and protects him...from deviating from what is good for the work.
It unites what he is with what his material is. It leads him to seek his own depths. Its purpose is
not his self-enhancement, his having fun or feeling good about himself. These are byproducts.
It aims solely towards bringing a new thing into existence in the truest manner possible. It is
about truth and, as such, has to do with ultimates and, as such, posits self-sacrifice and
consecration. As I see it, this is made to order for a Martin Puryear.[7]

Ever skeptical, with time Puryear took very seriously Sonneman's philosophical, even spiritual,
approach to the meaning of making art. This was the first of several instances in which Puryear
would find the processes of art identified as inseparable from the artist's own being: art as a sphere
of the psyche wherein an individual's physical and intellectual existence might be joined.

Puryear also studied painting with Sonneman:

From Martin's point of view his job was to represent as faithfully as good composition allowed
the still lifes or models (set up for the class to depart from). He could not relinquish the idea
of verisimilitude anymore than he could the skill and competence to attain it. Such control was
his achievement. O.K. But my job was to assist in removing obstacles that kept blood and guts
from being in the work.[8]

Even as a student Puryear possessed a strong will, and Sonneman struggled mightily to get him to
endow structure and space with as much intensity as he did exterior appearance, so that the "work
is flowing from an inner knowing of how things really are." Puryear would later describe the experience as a student in these terms: "As an art student I had come to grips with non-representational
art, which I did late and with a lot of difficulty. I didn't become a non-objective artist overnight. I went
through a series of stages, of learning how to see abstraction, and of giving up old habits."[9] Although
Puryear ultimately abandoned painting altogether, he did exhibit student work locally, on one occasion even winning a prize in the Maryland Regional Exhibition at the Baltimore Museum of Art.
While primarily a painter as an undergraduate, Puryear did attempt some sculpture in the months
before he graduated in June 1963, and he recalls being frustrated by the lack of equipment available
in the art department.[10]

Having grown up in a large family and having attended school in Washington, D.C., when
Puryear graduated in 1963 he had a desire to be independent and to travel. His search for new
horizons and a peaceful alternative to service in Viet Nam led him to the Peace Corps and to Sierra
Leone, on the west coast of Africa.[11] Although he taught art occasionally while in the Peace Corps,
his principal subjects were biology, French, and English, which he taught at a mission secondary
school. Puryear drew incessantly during his long stay in Africa. While a great many of these drawings
were subsequently damaged or destroyed, the artist still possesses a variety of works on paper that
he made in Sierra Leone. Detailed studies of trees, animals, and insects indicate that he retained his
youthful interest in plant and animal life, the last anatomically correct to the point of indicating
gender (see fig. 1). He made equally refined studies of his architectural surroundings, including the
chieftain's hut, the school in which he taught, and the "up garrett," as his own residence in Sierra

Fig. 2
Martin Puryear, *Untitled*, 1965
Ink on tan wove paper
13⅜ × 8⅝ in.
Collection of the artist

Fig. 3
Martin Puryear, *Untitled*, 1965
Ink and wash on tan wove paper
11⅝ × 8¹¹⁄₁₆ in.
Collection of the artist

Leone was called (see fig. 2). Typically these drawings were contained in letters to his parents for, without a camera, drawing was his only means to describe his surroundings to his family. These letters often included portraits of Puryear's students or residents of his village (see fig. 3). On the back of one such drawing, Puryear lamented the time spent in making detailed renderings. And, whereas some of these drawings are copiously detailed, others are radically simplified to a series of contours, suggesting the artist's first real embrace of abstraction (see fig. 4). As Puryear would later write, "When I left the country and went to Africa I think that was when I really earnestly in two-dimensional terms at least . . . found a way to deal with what I had recently discovered about abstraction."[12]

Although Puryear's skills as a woodworker were already fairly advanced when he left Washington (enough so that he made a guitar which could be disassembled, packed, and transported to Africa, where it was reassembled), he developed profound respect for the craftsmen he met in Sierra Leone. African carpenters built the furniture for the schoolhouse in which he taught, and gradually he met and observed them. Because only the hospital possessed electricity, the joinery and other traditional techniques that these carpenters practiced were accomplished with the ingenuity of hand and mind alone, and without the benefit of electric tools. Beyond the knowledge and skill he gained, Puryear was also introduced to a distinctly non-Western attitude toward craft. "In more traditional, more slowly evolving societies, there is always a downplaying of the craftsmen's ego. You spend time learning, in an almost menial way, initially, from an acknowledged authority, and you only earn the right to be an artist, with anything personal to invest in the work, through mastery."[13]

In 1966 Puryear completed his two-year assignment in Sierra Leone, and he felt no compulsion to return to the United States. He indulged a long-standing fascination with Scandinavia and moved to Stockholm. There were several reasons for this decision. First, Puryear was admitted to the Swedish Royal Academy of Art, and in 1967 he would receive a fellowship from the Scandinavian-American Foundation which facilitated his stay. Of at least equal importance, however, were the northern landscape and polar culture in general. Puryear's outdoor interests were always strong, and in the summer of 1967 he and his brother Michael worked for a month on the farm of a friend in northern Sweden in order to train for a long backpack trip above the Arctic circle in Swedish and Norwegian Lapland. On this trip and throughout his stay in Scandinavia, Puryear was tremendously impressed with the Arctic landscape as well as the basketry, quillwork, and other crafts of the Arctic.

Another reason for his move to Sweden was Puryear's admiration for the tradition of Scandinavian design and woodworking, which he now explored with great seriousness. "It seemed to me that Danish furniture had evolved out of a craft tradition into modern production without losing the vitality of the original precedent — or so it seemed to me from a distance. What appeared to be a lot of care and craftsmanship at close range turned out to be the result of very sophisticated technology."[14] Although somewhat disappointed by the realities of mechanized furniture production in Scandinavia, Puryear did discover craftsmen who worked on a very high level, totally independent of the values of mass production. During a visit to the Swedish Nationalmuseum, Puryear was greatly impressed by a small silver chest in pear and chestnut wood made only the year before by a cabinetmaker named James Krenov. After seeing Krenov's understated, immaculately conceived and crafted work in the museum, Puryear discovered publications on the man and his work in the library of the American consulate. In a burst of enthusiasm, he located Krenov's studio near Stockholm and visited him; ultimately he would spend some three weeks working informally as an assistant, carefully observing this master woodworker and learning whatever he could.[15]

Born in Siberia but raised in Seattle, Krenov had lived and worked in Stockholm since 1947. From that time he established a reputation as one of the preeminent cabinetmakers in the world, writing, lecturing, and teaching extensively. By his own estimate, Krenov's strength as a craftsman exists not in the originality of his forms but rather in his intuition with wood, his ability "to listen to but not dominate the wood."[16] He argues persuasively against heavyhanded and oversimplified work that apes the size, scale, and values of sculpture. Krenov's own work is generally small and somewhat delicate, with a particular emphasis on material texture and pattern, as well as on subtle, undulating linear form. And yet, it was not Krenov's own work that influenced Puryear, but rather the model that he provided. Krenov imbued his students with a profound love and respect for their chosen activity and for the materials of their labor. This all-embracing commitment to one's work, an attitude that Puryear had observed previously in Nell Sonneman, held that the individual's full involvement with the activity was reward enough; any explicit concerns with individualism and achievement were extrinsic to the life of the true artist/craftsman. Puryear has often described his debt to Krenov, noting that he "opened my eyes to an entirely new degree of commitment and sensitivity to materials."[17] Puryear's belief that an artist must master his hand before this dexterity might be transcended has remained a pillar of his thought.

Although Puryear had been admitted to the Swedish Royal Academy to study printmaking, he retained his love of wood craft and his principal activity soon became the making of three-dimensional objects. After making etchings during the day in the print shop, several of which were based on drawings he had made in Sierra Leone (see fig. 5), Puryear would spend his evenings in the sculpture studio working independently. Although he did some carving in wood, Puryear quickly determined to make sculpture through the methods of wood construction. "At a certain point I just put the building and the art impulse together. I decided that building was a legitimate way to make sculpture, that it wasn't necessary to work in the traditional methods of carving and casting."[18] It was at this point that Puryear gradually began to recognize a distinction in his own conception of art and craft. Although he retained great respect for the craft tradition that Krenov personified, he also concluded that the perfection of one's hand was not enough; once a level of manual accomplishment was reached, the heart and mind must press the hand to another level of making which might involve ideas.

To some degree, Puryear's subtle intellectual shift — away from craft and toward sculpture — was influenced by the vitality of the European art world. Stockholm was a particularly lively city in the 1960s, and the Moderna Museet, then under the dynamic leadership of Pontus Hulten, was among the preeminent museums in Europe, if not the world, devoted to contemporary art. The Royal Academy printmaking studio was located a short walk from the Moderna Museet, and Puryear

Fig. 4
Martin Puryear, *Untitled* (Joseph Momoh),
1965
Ink on tan wove paper
16½ x 11¼ in.
Collection of the artist

and his colleagues actually ate lunch in the museum cafeteria every day. For the first time since leaving Washington in 1964, Puryear engaged modern and contemporary art. This included renewed exposure to American Pop art, in the form of exhibitions of Claes Oldenburg (1966) and Andy Warhol (1968). At the Moderna Museet, Puryear also encountered and was greatly impressed by the work of a wide variety of other artists, among them Marcel Duchamp, Wifredo Lam, Antoni Tapies, Joseph Beuys, and the Swedish conceptualist and sculptor Carl Frederick Reuterwärd.[19] His curiosity about contemporary art piqued, Puryear attended the Venice Biennale before he returned to the United States in the fall of 1968. Although he found the American pavilion of only modest interest,

Fig. 5
Martin Puryear, *Gbows Gård*, 1966
Aquatint, engraving, and etching on white wove paper
18 × 23⅜ in.
Collection of the artist

Puryear was impressed by an international pavilion that included sculptures by Donald Judd, Tony Smith, and Robert Morris. Judd's *Untitled*, 1965 (fig. 6), had a particularly strong impact. As Puryear would later note, "At that point Minimalism became a strong clue for me about how powerful primary forms could be."[20]

Puryear's renewed exposure to contemporary art prompted strong curiosity about recent developments in art and culture in the United States. Beyond this, European art and culture began to suggest limits rather than the exhilaration that Puryear had first felt when he left Sierra Leone for Stockholm in 1966. He found that he missed the direct experience of American culture, which for several years had been transmitted to him secondhand. He missed the brash, vibrant energy of America, in contrast to European cultural life, which he found to be so heavily conditioned by history and the state.[21]

At the age of twenty-seven, Puryear returned to the United States, having made only a few sculptures and, at least on paper, only modest progress into the profession of art. And yet, he returned to the United States a mature, worldly, and highly focused individual, fully intent on his goal as an aspiring sculptor. His experiences abroad were distinctly unusual and this range of interests and knowledge would serve him well and set him apart from the vast majority of young artists whom he would encounter. Puryear's process of cultural assimilation — that is, the embrace of a wide variety of creative expression — had begun in his childhood. The opportunity to live in West Africa only enhanced Puryear's awareness of diverse forms of expression. Ultimately, his sculpture would bene-fit from this knowledge for he could call on an extensive variety of objects and visual ideas that he had either seen firsthand or read about.

Similarly, Puryear's experience with woodworkers — the carpenters of West Africa and the designers and craftsmen of Scandinavia — suggested an unusual approach to wood sculpture. When Puryear became seriously interested in the craft of wood, he explored it fully, acquiring both the philosophical understanding and the skills necessary to master wood. Yet once he recognized limits within the endeavor — the perception that craftsmanship alone does not yield art — he came to conceive of craft as a means rather than an end, and he set his sights instead on a sculpture that might be informed by the methods of craft. In so doing, Puryear recognized that sculpture in wood was made in one of two principal ways. Generally speaking, wood was carved, as Raoul Hague did, or it was assembled in the manner of Gabriel Kohn, or perhaps it was carved and assembled as in the case of Louise Bourgeois. Although Puryear was interested in the work of all three of these sculptors, and admired the work of Bourgeois in particular, he now began to pursue the processes of the joiner, the wheelwright, the cooper, and the patternmaker as sculptural techniques.[22] All require an entirely different form of studio practice and discipline than does carving or assemblage, and Puryear struck out on this course with relatively few models. This refusal to be cornered, a determi-nation to maintain his options, has become a particular characteristic and a strength of Puryear and his work. In time this would constitute a personal commitment to originality that would form one element of Puryear's modernism.

Following his return, Puryear was admitted to the graduate program in sculpture at Yale Univer-sity and he entered in the fall of 1969. The timing of this decision could not have been more fortuitous. Study at Yale put Puryear in close proximity to New York, which, in the late 1960s, was a hotbed of changing ideas concerning the very nature of sculpture. The most progressive direction in sculpture in the early and mid-1960s in New York was Minimalism, a movement canonized in a major exhibition, "Primary Structures: Younger American and British Sculptors," held at The Jewish Museum in 1966. Organized by Kynaston McShine, the exhibition identified a number of younger artists whose attitudes were new to contemporary sculpture. Influenced by the positivist attitudes of Constructivism, Minimalist sculptors such as Donald Judd, Carl Andre, Dan Flavin, and Robert Morris sought to activate and rigorously shape the spectator's experience of space. This was done through simple geometric forms that were often fabricated industrially and composed in serial arrangements. Rejecting embellishment, pedestals, open interior space, and human form and scale, all of which were thought to allude to emotive expression, these sculptors preferred an aggressively architectural scale, and color that was integrated into the fabrication process in order to achieve a unitary form and a direct confrontation with the viewer. These sculptors were generally university-trained, and Judd, Morris, and Flavin were all prolific writers on art. As a result, the level of discourse on sculpture in the mid- and late 1960s, particularly in the pages of *Artforum*, was often deafening.[23]

If Minimalism prevailed among sculptors working in New York in the mid-1960s, new challenges were close at hand. In fact, the onslaught of new ideas in sculpture was so direct, the pace of change so compelling, that by 1966 some of yesterday's Minimalists were advocating a much less formal approach. Robert Morris and Sol LeWitt, who wrote respectively on "anti-form" and "conceptual art" in the pages of *Artforum*,[24] were among the leaders of a less doctrinaire, more open-ended movement in sculpture. Throughout the remainder of the decade, these artists, along with Eva Hesse, Bruce Nauman, Richard Serra, and Robert Smithson, among numerous others, would challenge the prevailing notion of sculpture as based in solid objects. These artists viewed form as just one of many ideas that should infuse sculpture, and a wide variety of processes and materials were called into service, many of them impermanent. Throughout this work the bodily presence of the artist is felt — Serra pouring and splashing molten lead, Hesse feeding short strips of rubber through holes in a perforated cube, Bruce Nauman filming his own actions in the studio — and the nature of sculpture was emphatically changed. The proximity in time and place of these developments — which quickly came to be termed post-Minimalism — to Minimalism was so close that the first exhibition of this provocative new sensibility, "Eccentric Abstraction," was held in 1966, the same year as the "Primary Structures" show. Important exhibitions continued throughout the late 1960s, among them "Nine at Leo Castelli," a show organized by Robert Morris and held in an uptown warehouse in 1968, and "Anti-Illusion: Materials and Processes," staged at the Whitney Museum of American Art in 1969.[25]

Parallel to this new and liberating attitude toward materials and processes was the idea of taking sculpture outside the gallery, the museum, and even outside the city, to locations in the natural and often distant landscape. Earthworks evolved in the mid-1960s as well, with artists such as Morris, Smithson, Michael Heizer, and Walter DeMaria, as well as Richard Long in England, making their mark in nature and apart from what was beginning to be seen as a constricting commercial environment. In short, Puryear's return to the United States coincided with some of the most compelling and radical developments in the history of modern sculpture, and Minimalism, post-Minimalism, and Earthworks, which Puryear experienced in the museums and galleries of New York and in the pages of journals such as *Artforum*, would all play roles in the development of his thinking around 1970.

At Yale, Puryear found a variety of options open to him. The dominant artists on the faculty were James Rosati and Al Held, but of equal or greater importance to Puryear during these years were several visiting instructors: Serra, Morris, and Salvatore Scarpitta, among others. Rosati, a sculptor of the Abstract Expressionist generation, who worked with massive, muscular forms, was the chairman of the sculpture program, yet he was absent a great deal because he was thoroughly involved with the industrial fabrication of a group of large steel sculptures. While Rosati provided an

Fig. 6
Donald Judd (American, b. 1928), *Untitled*, 1965
Light cadmium red enamel on cold-rolled steel
15⅝ in. x 11 ft. 6 in. x 9 ft. 9 in.
Collection of the artist

exemplary if somewhat distant presence as a working sculptor, Puryear maintained a dialogue with Held, this despite the fact that he undertook no painting courses at Yale. During Puryear's Yale years, Held expressed interest in his work, and he later visited him in the studio Puryear established in Brooklyn in 1973.[26]

In contrast to Rosati stood Serra and Morris. Serra's work with rubber, neon, cast and molten lead, and other nontraditional materials emphasized an extremely direct approach to the processes of sculpture. Particularly in his early work, Serra personified Puryear's rejection of pure craftsman-ship alone; that is, the notion that "skills alone are not enough," indeed, that the progressive artist must be "suspicious of skills."[27] In contrast to the physicality of Serra's often blue-collar methods, Robert Morris exemplified a greater conceptual awareness, that held that attitudes toward artistic activity outweighed matters of style. This more theoretical approach also appealed to Puryear, who had come to realize that his experience in Europe had induced a more intellectual approach to art, one that effectively balanced his commitment to craft. If Serra reinforced Puryear's natural inclination toward direct, physical involvement with materials and making, Morris's wide-ranging activities rein-forced the conceptual interests that Puryear had developed while in Europe. To some degree the contrast between Serra and Morris was reflected in the work of the Yale students. Puryear recalls the clear division that existed between "white-collar" and "blue-collar" artists; that is, between artists who worked with ideas and those who worked with their hands. Not surprisingly, Puryear found himself in neither camp, believing that his conceptual interests were not at odds with his passion for making. Although Puryear enjoyed the dialogue, both in the New York art press and at Yale, he rejected the need to take sides and began to establish a personal definition of what his sculpture could be.[28]

Puryear's student work was wide-ranging and experimental. He was working primarily with arrangements of milled wood which were stacked and pinned in place by the force of gravity, and bearing titles such as *Hemlock Load, Oak Cast* and *Oak Wood Pile* (both 1972). Both of these works were included in Puryear's first American solo exhibition, held at the Henri 2 Gallery in Washington early in 1972, only a few months after he received his graduate degree from Yale. Although these sculptures were later destroyed and are known only from poor reproductions, they were rough-cut but standard lengths of wood, stacked into standing and often frontal geometric configurations. Writing in *The Washington Post*, Paul Richard described Puryear's first show as "tons of timbers, rough lengths of oak and fir and hemlock, stacked and spliced and simply organized by gravity and fric-tion."[29] And, indeed, throughout this early work one senses Puryear handling, cutting, and stacking the wood. If Puryear's experience of Judd's work had suggested an early interest in Minimalism, he had now moved on to a more direct, process-oriented approach to sculpture, in which the physical involvement of the sculptor was central. Rather than having his work fabricated to precise specifica-tions, Puryear, like the early Richard Serra, was involved in every step of the process of making, and his sculptures bore the clear imprint of his hand.

Puryear's exhibition in Washington occurred after he had already begun teaching at Fisk Uni-versity, a black college in Nashville, where he would live until 1973. He enjoyed close friendships and

Fig. 7
Martin Puryear, *Bound Cone*, 1973
Oak and rope
70 in. high
Mrs. William Martin, Nashville, Tennessee

21

a spirit of community at Fisk, without losing sight of art-world developments in New York and Washington. Puryear's work changed rather dramatically, albeit temporarily, in Nashville, for he not only rejected milled wood in favor of natural lengths of pine, poplar, oak, and Osage orange, he also employed a whole range of nontraditional materials: rope, leather, concrete, and even rawhide which he scraped and cured himself. As these materials might suggest, Puryear's sculptures briefly took on a decidedly funky look, rejecting Minimalist clarity in favor of a playful informality: toggles joined with lengths of rope arranged freely on the floor; stuffed calfskins mounted offhandedly on the wall; a long, narrow cone of wood cut in thirds and leaned end-to-end in the shape of the letter *N*. Writing in *Art in America*, on the occasion of Puryear's second Henri 2 Gallery show in 1973, David Bourdon described the work as "a dozen or so carefully crafted objects in an abstract surrealist mode ... Puryear works with wood, rope and leather, traditional materials that he converts into a fugitive form of surrealism, a nonrepresentational but highly referential type of abstraction."[30] Although this group of works initially seems aberrant compared to the work that followed, several elements of Puryear's later work appeared here for the first time. For example, a small, free-standing, half-circular arc made of laminated strips of willow wood was Puryear's first bent-wood sculpture, a process that the artist would employ repeatedly later in the decade; a poplar cone painted in bands of copper, green, blue, and yellow, and towering over a minute egg-shaped form below presages Puryear's later engagement with color and his contrast of large- and small-scale form. Perhaps the most impressive work was *Bound Cone*, a trim oak spire standing just under six feet high (fig. 7). Split lengthwise from top to bottom, this laceration is healed by a rope carefully wound around the middle of the torso and then pinned in the split above and below, giving the sculpture a feeling of great physical tension. The contrast between inside and out and the allusion to human scale would both become crucial in later work. Although Puryear would continue to employ materials such as rawhide — for example, in the sculpture *Rawhide Cone*, 1974 (cat. no. 1) — and his work would always reveal the process of its making, the sculptures of the early 1970s remain Puryear's most informal to date.

Puryear left Fisk in 1973 and, after a summer in Washington, established a studio in a warehouse in the Williamsburg section of Brooklyn. Although he taught at the University of Maryland between 1974 and 1978 (commuting to the campus in College Park each week), he spent the majority of his time working in New York in his first studio space adequate for making sculpture. Puryear welcomed the renewed challenge of New York with the feedback and competition from other artists that this engendered. His first mature works were made at this time, pieces that reflect a consistent and accomplished handling of wood while simultaneously addressing a range of sculptural problems. For example, *Bask*, 1976 (cat. no. 3), is a low-slung, softly curving form, measuring only twelve inches high but an expansive twelve feet long. Puryear considers the work among his most accomplished early sculptures; technically he had found a way to make milled wood swell without resorting to carving. *Bask* possesses a sweeping silhouette yet it is also strongly volumetric, and although it is unitary in form, it is rich in biomorphic allusion.[31] *Bask* clearly refers to nature, perhaps the curvature of the earth or the dark silhouette of a whale quietly parting the water's surface. Evocative and even

Fig. 8
Martin Puryear, *Cedar Lodge*, 1977
Red cedar, fir, and rawhide
18 ft. high x 16 ft. 6 in. diameter
Installed at The Corcoran Gallery of Art,
Washington, D.C., 1977

22

Fig. 9
Martin Puryear, *Rune Stone*, 1966
Aquatint, engraving, and etching on white
wove paper
23½ × 18¼ in.
Collection of the artist

lyrical, *Bask* seems less manmade than natural, in much the same way Jean Arp's sculpture seems to spring forth, fully formed, from nature. By contrast, *Circumbent*, 1976 (cat. no. 4), is a sculpture in two pieces: a gently undulating semicircle of laminated wood, stained a deep red and bent slightly out of plane, and a standing vertical support in an even deeper blue. As Puryear notes, the vertical seems to bend slightly under the weight of the curved element, and the title *Circumbent* contains several punning references to weight and repose (recumbent), and to curves and the process of bending wood (bent and circumvent).[32]

Bask and *Circumbent*, both made in 1976, were Puryear's strongest works up to that point. His work was attracting increasing attention, and his studio, his apartment, and a small adjoining room that he was using as a display space were all full of sculptures in process or already complete. And yet, with all these positive developments, while away from his studio on February 1, 1977, Puryear "had a premonition of a fire in my studio — the ultimate disaster for a wood sculptor."[33] He returned home to find his worst fear had become reality: a savage fire had destroyed his Brooklyn studio and apartment along with all of his books and tools and most of his possessions. Only a few sculptures survived: *Bask*, *Circumbent*, and another work of 1976 titled *Stripling* (cat. no. 5), as well as elements of an unfinished work that would soon be completed and titled *Some Tales* (cat. no. 2).

A catastrophe of this magnitude can have disastrous consequences for an artist. The loss of a body of work and a smoothly functioning studio space can be a paralyzing setback, throwing an artist off-course for a long period of time. In Puryear's case the fire had precisely the opposite effect. As he described it, "The fire was followed by a period of grieving and then by an incredible lightness, freedom, and mobility."[34] And, in fact, a flurry of activity followed almost immediately. Jane Livingston, a curator at the Corcoran Gallery of Art in Washington, D.C., offered Puryear an exhibition that coming summer. Still teaching at the University of Maryland, Puryear quickly moved to Washington where he established a temporary studio. It was there that the works for the Corcoran exhibition were completed.

The first work was the aforementioned *Some Tales*, on which Puryear had been working since 1975. The graphic character of *Circumbent* was now expanded exponentially, as *Some Tales* is composed of six spoke-shaved wooden saplings and a rugged saw-toothed device, the whole measuring nearly thirty feet in length. Within the horizontal flow of the piece, great differences appear. Of the five saplings, most were spliced together or otherwise joined to form a lyrical, even musical, composition. By contrast, the heavy beam is notched in such a way that the teeth and the points shift in orientation from left to right — a subtle aspect that belies the otherwise rugged look of the form. The powerful horizontal thrust of the individual elements, combined with the title, suggests a narrative; Puryear himself likened the piece to a *quipu*, a mnemonic object used by the Incas to calculate and record.[35]

The other major work, which Puryear brought to fruition in the galleries of the Corcoran, was *Cedar Lodge*, an enormous environmental structure (fig. 8). Installed in a two-story gallery at the Corcoran, *Cedar Lodge* was a sculpture to be seen from the outside, but also to be entered. It consisted of an armature of five laminated Douglas fir rings with the whole faced with red cedar slats. Lashed across the opening near the top was a light-admitting cowhide cupola that translated the Corcoran skylight into an amber glow inside the sculpture. Although *Cedar Lodge* was dismantled and destroyed following the exhibition, numerous visitors and critics commented on the mysteriousness of this consecrated and quite secret space. For an artist suddenly made homeless, *Cedar Lodge* suggests a kind of spiritual center. Taken together, *Some Tales* and *Cedar Lodge* possess a depth of allusion as yet unseen in Puryear's work. One senses untold thoughts and feelings in these sculptures, from an artist increasingly capable of projecting himself into his work without revealing himself in any explicit manner.

Puryear has often considered exhibitions as implying a moment of closure on a period of time or a body of work. He has also been somewhat peripatetic ("I think of moving as a kind of saving grace," he noted recently[36]), and following the fire and the Corcoran exhibition, in 1978, he resigned his position at the University of Maryland and moved to Chicago, in order to accept a position at the University of Illinois, Chicago. Themes of personal strength, mobility, and flight would pervade Puryear's work for several years. While still in Washington in early 1978, Puryear made a piece titled *Self* (cat. no. 7), a dark, monolithic-looking form reminiscent of prints he had made while a student in Stockholm a decade earlier (see fig. 9). And, indeed, *Self* feels massive and heavy, as if to suggest the weight and solidity of stone planted firmly in the earth. Yet this is an illusion, as Puryear built the form in thin layers over a hollow core. He has described the piece in the following terms: "It looks as though it might have been created by erosion, like a rock worn by sand and weather until the angles are all gone. *Self* is all curve except where it meets the floor at an abrupt angle. It's meant to be a visual notion of the self, rather than any particular self — the self as a secret entity, as a secret, hidden place."[37]

Fig. 10
Inner Mongolia, *Yurt*, 1923–24
Peabody Museum, Harvard University,
Cambridge, Massachusetts

Fig. 11
Martin Puryear, *Where the Heart Is (Sleeping Mews)*, 1990
Mixed-media
Yurt: 18 ft. diameter
Installed at the Museum of Fine Arts, Boston, 1990

Fig. 12
Martin Puryear, *Where the Heart Is (Sleeping Mews)* (detail), 1990

Other works address the idea of self in other ways. In August 1977 Puryear completed the framework of a yurt, a collapsible, wooden dwelling standing ten feet high and eighteen feet in diameter. Developed in Central Asia by seminomadic peoples at least as early as the thirteenth century, yurts are trellised wooden structures capped by low, arching conical roofs, and covered by a number of layers of felt (see fig. 10). Although portable, as befitting the need to travel, a heavy wooden door was usually employed at night. Puryear has exhibited his yurt, which he titled *Where the Heart Is (Sleeping Mews)*, on three separate occasions — in 1981, 1987, and 1990 — varying its external appearance and contents on each occasion. For example, Puryear has included objects such as a stove, a kettle, a lamp, and a small bronze chair similar to those employed as chieftains' chairs in West Africa (see figs. 25, 26).[38] While these objects have varied, one constant has been the inclusion of nearly abstract sculpted birds in various materials. For example, when the piece was first exhibited in Seattle's and/or gallery in 1981, Puryear included two birds, one inside the yurt and one perched on a ledge mounted on the gallery wall. Puryear later described these forms as a reference to ornithology:

> The installation also consisted of some quotations from a Russian ornithologist who had written a book on a particular bird of prey that's fascinated me for a long time. The bird is called the gyrfalcon, and has a rather romantic history. It is the largest of all falcons, and appears only in Arctic regions of the globe: Lapland, Siberia, Alaska, Iceland, and Northern Canada. The gyrfalcon is found in different color phases, from pure white in Greenland to nearly solid black in Labrador. There are various theories advanced about the color phases, regarding whether the plumage differences represent subspecies or racial differences and why they're distributed as they are geographically. This interested me as another kind of metaphor.[39]

Puryear's youthful obsession with falconry now assumed rather complex implications. Beyond the apparent depth of his knowledge on the subject, falconry clearly suggests for the artist a symbol of spiritual liberation. Beyond the abilities of the falconer, who acts as a surrogate parent to the bird, coaxing it to maturity and gaining satisfaction from the exploits of his charge, the falcon must possess remarkable intelligence, discipline, and independent will, for it cannot be directed to hunt and must develop and demonstrate all its skills within a realm of freedom.

Puryear's interest in falconry extends to representations of these magnificent birds throughout the history of art. This includes his knowledge of the work of John James Audubon, which Puryear studied in his youth and which helped inspire his early desire to become a wildlife illustrator. In 1977, the same year as the fire, Puryear saw a seventeenth-century Mughal painting of a falcon at the Museum of Fine Arts in Boston; this image stayed with him for over a decade and it became the inspiration for the most recent exhibition of *Where the Heart Is*, which occurred at that museum in 1990. For that installation Puryear filled both the yurt and the surrounding gallery space and walls with a whole range of highly abstracted falcon effigies, evoking a deeply personal natural environment (figs. 11, 12).

The yurt has provided Puryear with a sculptural form rich with associative possibilities. Unlike Mario Merz's igloos, the Italian artist's signature form emblematic of his despair at the fragility of

Fig. 13
Mario Merz (Italian, b. 1925), *For L.A. All for the cypress, all for the crocodile, all for the five chairs* (detail), 1989
Mixed-media
Installed at The Museum of Contemporary Art, Los Angeles, 1989

Fig. 14
Martin Puryear, *Equation for Jim Beckwourth*, 1980
Pitch pine, oak, vines, rawhide, earth, and grass
Dimensions variable
Installed at the Museum of Contemporary Art, Chicago, 1980

civilization (see fig. 13), Puryear's sculpture is clearly a more directly personal work. Indeed, the sculptor's punning use of the word "mews" in the title, on the one hand prosaically referring to the cages used for moulting hawks and, on the other, its more evocative homonym "muse," suggests Puryear's conception of the yurt as a surrogate spiritual studio during the period after the fire.[40]

In time, Puryear's consistent association of the yurt and falconry would expand these implications. Dualities are apparent in each: the yurt provides a physical and psychological base for man within a seminomadic existence, and falconry is based in the discipline of a bird of prey to operate with extraordinary freedom and vitality while retaining its connection to the falconer. The ongoing correlation of falconry and the yurt in Puryear's art suggests a continuing search for just such a spiritual balance — between freedom and mobility on the one hand, and the stability of a home to provide physical and psychological sustenance on the other.

Beyond this, Puryear's particular fascination with the Arctic gyrfalcon — a species that possesses plumage ranging from pure white to deep black and that was once erroneously considered racially diverse but is now regarded as a single species — is also important. For Puryear who, as a black artist, has often crossed ethnic and cultural boundaries, the gyrfalcon possesses obvious metaphorical interest. Beyond this, Puryear counts among his heroes little-known historical figures whose lives reflect similar possibilities. With his love of the Arctic, Puryear enjoys reciting the remarkable story of Matthew Henson, an accomplished black explorer who accompanied Admiral Robert Peary on his many expeditions in search of the North Pole. In contrast to the imperious and often manipulative Peary, who employed Henson to complete much of the difficult work while claiming all their discoveries as his alone, Henson acted as an indispensable force on the expeditions, learning the languages and befriending the peoples of the Arctic and, according to some accounts, perhaps even discovering the North Pole himself.[41]

Contemporaneous with the early evolution of his yurt, Puryear was also celebrating a remarkable and little-known figure in American history: James Beckwourth. Born in the late eighteenth century, the son of a white man and a mulatto slave woman, Beckwourth was manumitted in the Louisiana Territory, and subsequently worked on various expeditions in the West. He apparently married several Native American women, settling for a time with one of them, and he was even made a chief of the Crow Indians. Eventually he traveled to California in search of gold, participated in the Mexican War, and served as a guide and translator for United States troops in the Cheyenne War.[42]

Like Henson's, Beckwourth's life offers a distant but compelling metaphor of existence based on cultural adaptability and personal daring and mobility, in which boundaries of race and culture are transcended. As Puryear recently noted, "I often think of his migration from the humblest of origins to a kind of kingliness."[43] That Puryear admires Beckwourth's biography is evident: in 1978 he titled a new installation *Some Lines for Jim Beckwourth* (cat. no. 8), and he subsequently integrated this piece into another work, *Equation for Jim Beckwourth*, which was exhibited at the Museum of Contemporary Art, Chicago, in 1980 (fig. 14). This work, measuring nearly seventy feet in length, was composed of several parts: to the right, the aforementioned *Some Lines for Jim Beckwourth* (six long, twisted rawhide thongs) and the second version of *Rawhide Cone* (cat. no. 1) — the original was lost in the fire and a copy was fabricated for the MCA show. To the left, Puryear composed another series of horizontal wall-mounted elements, this time a group of saplings. Uniting the two halves of the "equation" was a long sapling that stretched from left to right. Puryear placed only two elements on the floor of this narrow gallery space: a vertical division, and a heavy wooden cone that bears a top layer of sod — a work later exhibited separately and titled *For Beckwourth* (cat. no. 13). *Equation for Jim Beckwourth* was thus composed of two sides: one made of wood, the other of hide with red, black, and white remnants of cattle hair. Although developed from different materials, the two halves of the equation "were alike in that both halves included helical lines placed on the wall at eye level like writing."[44] If this linguistic or narrative aspect recalls the earlier work *Some Tales*, *Equation for Jim Beckwourth* also possessed a tactile quality not unlike the Inca *quipu* or even the Christian rosary.[45]

Beyond this, the MCA installation was now more complex sculpturally. Whereas Puryear originally had made *Rawhide Cone* to be placed directly on the floor, and would exhibit it in this manner on several occasions in the future, here it was affixed to the wall. In linking it to the sod-roofed object on the floor, Puryear for the first time sought an unusual tension between wall-mounted and three-dimensional sculpture.

Puryear was finding a variety of methods through which to express the contrasting notions of mobility and stability. While *Where the Heart Is* is an environment, an architectural entity containing literal references to such ideas, *Equation for Jim Beckwourth* bore these implications through the lateral progression of the piece from side to side. In 1982 Puryear made another piece that treated this same idea, but in a very different way. This is *Sanctuary* (cat. no. 17), a wall-mounted sculpture consisting of an open box, connected to two thick branches that extend down and attach to the axle of a wheel. *Sanctuary* is a hybrid sculptural form relying for support on both the floor and the wall. The sculpture brings stability and mobility into a taut relationship: the box, made of milled lumber and securely mounted above, versus the kinetic potential of the wheel below. This link between stability and motion and, in sculptural terms, between relief and sculpture in the round, is now concentrated in a single complex form. As Puryear has noted, all these works — the yurt in its evolving forms, the Beckwourth pieces, and *Sanctuary* — deal "with mobility, and a kind of escapism, of survival through flight."[46]

In sum, these works trace Puryear's development of a theme — the vitality of the spirit when freed of limits — through a number of references and forms. On the one hand, diverse objects, activities, ideas, and historical figures such as the yurt, falconry, the box and the wheel, and James Beckwourth, all reflect this remarkably rich notion. Beyond this, Puryear's maturity as a sculptor is seen in his ability to concentrate often complex conceptual and visual ideas within a single, multilayered form. Yet Puryear did this without evolving a narrow formal vocabulary, for he was finding that different creative pursuits — architectural, relief, and three-dimensional — all had a place in his work, and each could be called upon should the occasion suggest it. A modernist rather than a formalist, Puryear was coming to recognize the importance of exploring, developing, and then retaining all his options, both sculpturally and thematically.

Working in Chicago in the late 1970s and early 1980s, Puryear also concentrated on a large body of wall-mounted sculpture and a number of outdoor projects. His first major outdoor sculpture — *Box and Pole* (figs. 15, 16) — was developed in the summer of 1977 while Puryear was living in Washington. Constructed for Artpark, in Lewiston, New York, *Box and Pole* consists of two parts: a four-and-a-half-foot-square cube constructed of dovetailed beams, and a one-hundred-foot-high pole, made of two trees spliced together and shaved nearly to a point at the top. Beyond the obvious contrast of shapes, Puryear explicitly contrasted wood in its natural state and appearance with manmade, milled lumber. While the pole possesses the form, scale, and upward infinite reach of Constantin Brancusi's *Endless Column*, the box, with its extreme concentration and compression, "is very much about artifact; the pole shows how wood appears in nature, tall and straight and upright. The box sits just under eye level so the average viewer can feel superior to it, while the pole towers

Fig. 15
Martin Puryear constructing *Box* (for *Box and Pole*) at Artpark, Lewiston, New York, 1977

Fig. 16
Martin Puryear, *Box and Pole*, 1977
Canadian hemlock and southern
yellow pine
Box: 54 x 54 x 54 in.
Pole: 100 ft. high
Installed at Artpark, Lewiston,
New York, 1977

Fig. 17
Martin Puryear, *Equivalents*, 1979
Canadian hemlock
Box: 54 x 54 x 54 in.
Cone: 87½ x 75 x 75 in.
Installed at Wave Hill, Bronx,
New York, 1979

above and dwarfs him."[47] Larger than an object, smaller than a monument, the box posits a scale for outdoor art that is resolutely human, while the pole "activates the sky, the clouds, and the surrounding space,"[48] thereby claiming the vastness of space for the sculpture.

The issue of scale, as well as a distinction between formal and what might be termed contextual or environmental concerns, would become central to Puryear's outdoor sculpture. Puryear has completed a number of outdoor projects, some of which, like *Box and Pole*, are temporary installations composed of durable structures of clear, geometric form which were appropriate for siting out-of-doors. One of these, *Equivalents* (fig. 17), in which the cube (the same one made for Artpark) and the cone possessed the same volume, was installed at Wave Hill in Bronx, New York, in 1979.

Others, such as *Sentinel*, 1982 (see p. 154), a mortar and fieldstone sculpture installed on the campus of Gettysburg College, translate the powerful, compressed form of *Self* to a public setting. Whether temporary or permanent, all expand on ideas that existed in Puryear's work, thereby revealing the artist's perception that some outdoor sculptural projects provide vehicles for extending his studio work to exterior settings and scale.

In contrast to these sculptures, in which Puryear tested his studio solutions outdoors, and focused on establishing relationships of scale, in the early 1980s the sculptor completed another body of outdoor work with somewhat different implications. These might be described as more environmental or contextual in nature, and several even have functional applications, for example, *Knoll for NOAA* (fig. 18), begun in 1981 for the National Oceanic and Atmospheric Administration (NOAA) in Seattle and completed in 1983.[49] For the Seattle project, Puryear responded to the

Fig. 18
Martin Puryear, *Knoll for NOAA*, 1981
(built 1983)
Concrete and plantings
Knoll: 45 ft. diameter × 54 in. high
Western Regional Center, National Oceanic and Atmospheric Administration, Seattle, Washington

Fig. 19
Lapland, *Njâllâ*
From Roberto Bosi, *The Lapps*, trans. James Cadell (1960; rpt. Westport, Connecticut: Greenwood Press, 1976), fig. 21

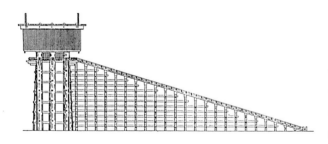

Fig. 20
Japan, *Honden*
From Yasutada Watanabe, *Shinto Art: Ise and Izumo Shrines*, trans. Robert Ricketts (New York: Weatherhill/Heibonsha, 1974), fig. 71

feelings of the NOAA employees, who requested an outdoor social space that would capitalize on the site's splendid views of Lake Washington. As Puryear later noted, "I felt it was part of the spirit of the whole program to do more than simply make an object." He describes his *Knoll for NOAA* as an "object-place,"[50] which Puryear quite consciously sited apart from the work of the other commissioned artists, Siah Armajani, Scott Burton, Doug Hollis, and George Trakas. The piece consists of a large concrete dome articulated by an incised spiral; surrounding the dome and corresponding to its curve are four stone benches and several trees, which, when fully grown, should provide shelter for the site.

Also in 1981 Puryear proposed *Pavilion-in-the-Trees* (fig. 21), an as-yet-unrealized project for Philadelphia. Functional suggestiveness remains an element of Puryear's outdoor work here as well, as the design calls for a raised platform amidst the trees in a Philadelphia park. This elevated enclosure is to be covered by a domed and gridded redwood roof, and will be reached by a sloping ramp. The unusual manner in which the form is elevated on poles and thus separated from the ground suggests two rather distant architectural analogues. One is a *njâllâ* — a Lapp storage structure consisting of a wooden cabin mounted high atop a pole and reached by a ladder in the form of a notched tree trunk (see fig. 19). The other is the Japanese *honden*, a Shinto sanctuary raised on a series of wooden posts and entered by a diagonal ramp (see fig. 20).[51] Puryear is well aware of the hybrid nature of his design, which crosses established boundaries separating sculpture and architecture, and between pure form and function: "Given that categories are blurred these days I would still say that it's a public amenity, designed by a sculptor, which tries to invest a public facility with a bit more poetry than it otherwise might have."[52]

Puryear's characterization begs comparison with contemporary notions of public sculpture and of site-specificity. This term gained currency in the 1960s, when it was introduced by Minimalists to suggest that the location of a sculpture was integral to its form and meaning. The career and attitudes of Richard Serra have come to characterize this approach, which holds that the "experience of the work is inseparable from the place in which the work resides. Apart from that condition any experience of the work is a deception."[53] At its most potent, this view suggests that a sculpture may retrieve a poor site, and artists such as Morris and Smithson all took on projects involving ecological reclamation. Similarly, Serra hoped that his ill-fated *Tilted Arc* would improve an unfortunate site in Lower Manhattan: "It will cross the entire space, blocking the view from the street to the courthouse and vice versa. The placement of the sculpture will change the space of the plaza. After the piece is created, the space will be understood primarily as a function of the sculpture."[54] However, a decidedly unselfconscious view of site-specificity also exists. In contrast to the willfulness of Serra stands the Englishman Richard Long, who advocates a far more personal and understated view of sculpture. Based in his own act of walking, seeing, and feeling in a particular location, Long acts merely to record the experience by organizing the stones or sticks he finds there, or by making drawings, maps, or photographs. Rather than an attempt to shape an environment permanently, for Long, site-specificity consists of "using the land with respect and freedom. I use materials, ideas, movement and time to express a whole view of my art in the world. I hope to make images and

Fig. 21
Martin Puryear, Model for *Pavilion-in-the-Trees*, 1981
Wood
17¼ x 11⅞ x 29³⁄₁₆ in.
Collection of the artist

ideas which resonate in the imagination, which mark the earth and the mind . . . . I like the idea of using the land without possessing it."[55]

Puryear's approach to outdoor art differs from that of both Serra and Long. While possessing a strong will, he would never impose himself or his work on a site and its visitors, nor would he be satisfied simply to record his experience of a place that moved him. Puryear's outdoor work is characterized by his desire to have visitors experience a site in a more profound manner; his is a humanistic ambition for public art and experience. It is perhaps no accident that *Box and Pole* and *Knoll for NOAA* recall Brancusi's work at Tirgu Jiu. Indeed, the resemblance is as much conceptual as it is formal. Brancusi's ensemble of three major sculptures — the *Table of Silence*, the *Gate of the Kiss*, and the *Endless Column*, all linked by the Avenue of the Heroes — exists as a zone consecrated by sculpture, a pathway that evokes a feeling of recollection and thoughtfulness.[56] Time is a key element here, for just as Brancusi's work must be experienced through the process of walking, throughout his public as well as his studio work, Puryear encourages the viewer to slow down and reflect quietly.

Without question, Puryear's most original and remarkable outdoor project to date is *Bodark Arc*, a vast environmental site sculpture completed for the Nathan Manilow Sculpture Park in 1982 (figs. 22-25).[57] Located south of Chicago on the campus of Governors State University, the park includes important works by Mark di Suvero, Mary Miss, and Bruce Nauman, among others, all sited in an enormous, unlandscaped prairie environment. In essence *Bodark Arc* is demarcated by a semi-circular path carved from the grass, a low bridge over an existing pond, and a hedgerow of Osage orange trees. The title derives from these trees, as "bodark" is a distortion of the French *bois d'arc* (bow wood), and thus a reference to the bows that Native Americans made from this same Osage

Overleaf:
Fig. 22
Martin Puryear, *Bodark Arc*, 1982
Wood, asphalt, and bronze
392 ft. diameter
The Nathan Manilow Sculpture Park, Governors State University, University Park, Illinois

Fig. 23
Martin Puryear, *Bodark Arc: Bridge* (detail),
1982

Fig. 24
Martin Puryear, *Bodark Arc: Arch* (detail),
1982

orange wood. A pair of remarkable coincidences exist here: Puryear had been fascinated by archery as a child when he made his own bows from Osage orange, and he had also made sculptures from the material when he lived in Nashville, where the trees are also plentiful. Beyond the path, the bridge, and the stand of trees, Puryear added only two objects to the site: a simple wooden gateway that stands near the point where the paths meet near the pond, and a cast of the small bronze chair that had been installed previously within *Where the Heart Is (Sleeping Mews)*, and which is reminiscent of West African chieftains' chairs (see fig. 26).

Because of its location, *Bodark Arc* is best known through reproductions, in particular, from a remarkable aerial view of the site (fig. 22). And yet, although spectacular, this view is ultimately misleading. Seen from above, the sculpture seems extremely linear, like *Circumbent*, or perhaps *M. Bastion Bouleversé* (fig. 27), a wall-mounted sculpture Puryear made for the 1979 Whitney Biennial. This work consisted of a field of small objects — several of them miniature versions of existing Puryear sculptures — mounted high on a wall and circumscribed by a long, nearly circular sapling. *Bouleversé* derives from the French verb *bouleverser*, meaning to overthrow or overturn, and Puryear's sculpture readily suggests an aerial view. In fact, the artist has described it as "more or less about the idea of presenting an aerial view as if the viewer is a bird soaring over occupied territory."[58]

If a superficial formal relationship exists between *Bodark Arc* and *M. Bastion Bouleversé*, the experience of the two works could hardly be more different. While the Whitney installation was seen frontally, with the allusion to an aerial view readily apparent, *Bodark Arc* is discovered through the lengthy process of traversing the prairie landscape. Furthermore, if Puryear's principal concern as a sculptor has been with objects, *Bodark Arc* stands apart, for its essential power resides in the individual's discovery of a landscape that is virtually free of manmade forms.

> The campus is on the grounds of an old farm, and the character of the farm is still strong — fields, hedgerows, and meadow ponds. It seemed best to turn the whole thing inside out, and make the objectness of my work disappear — to create as different an experience from the other works at Governors State University as I could, and to put a break in the chain of experiences that the other sculptures set up. The site I landed on feels much more isolated than it really is; it's almost magical. It occurred to me that within its limited radius there was a whole range of the local ecology. I used a long arcing path to pull you through 180 degrees of very different landscape realms — a little swamp with cattails, a pond which you cross over on a narrow curving bridge, all beginning and ending in the arcade of tree branches beneath the hedgerow of osage orange, or bodark trees, which is very secluded.[59]

Puryear obviously has a love of vast, open, and uncluttered places. His willingness to make *Bodark Arc* an emblem of understatement may relate to a trip he took the previous year to Alaska. With his brother Michael, Puryear canoed the length of the Noatak River, a location so remote that the two brothers had to be flown in by a bush pilot in a prop plane. Puryear recalls the vast wilderness, without even a trace of human presence, and his own craving for structure within the free landscape. And yet, beyond the bridge and the path, Puryear added to *Bodark Arc* only the gate and the chair. Puryear is a student of chairs, and he possesses a large library and wide-ranging knowledge of

Fig. 25
Martin Puryear, *Bodark Arc: Chair* (detail), 1982

Fig. 26
Mano, Liberia, *Chieftain's chair*, 1936–38
Wood, 18 in. high
The American Museum of Natural History, New York

Fig. 27
Martin Puryear, *M. Bastion Bouleversé*,
1978–79
Hickory, Alaskan yellow cedar, and deerskin
17 ft. × 18 ft. × 24 inches
Installed at the Whitney Museum of
American Art, New York, 1979

the history of the form. Beyond this, he has made many chairs himself, most often for his own enjoyment and use in his home and studio. In contrast to *Knoll for NOAA*, which acts to facilitate social interaction by creating a situation for group seating, Puryear here offered only a single low seat. *Bodark Arc* was obviously conceived for individual experience, emphasizing seclusion and personal discovery in nature, and the chair forms the single stationary moment in the experience of the work, a resting place at the focal point of the plan.

The other additive element is the simple arched wooden gateway, which stands near the intersection of the radius and the half-circle near the pond. Although gates traditionally suggest moments of ceremonial passage — indeed, Puryear's gate recalls a Japanese *torii*, the gateway to Shinto shrines — its unselfconscious form and human scale reinforce the experience of the isolated site as individual and highly personal. The gate of *Bodark Arc* contrasts dramatically with *Ampersand*, a far more public gateway that Puryear would complete six years later for the Minneapolis Sculpture Garden,

Fig. 28
Martin Puryear, *Ampersand*, 1987–88
Granite
East column: 13 ft. 7 in. × 36 in. × 36 in.
West column: 13 ft. 11 in. × 36 in. × 38 in.
Walker Art Center, Minneapolis, Gift of
Margaret and Angus Wurtele, 1988

directly across from the Walker Art Center (fig. 28). Whereas the two large gray granite columns of *Ampersand* offer the numerous visitors a formal introduction to a park devoted to sculpture, the *Bodark Arc* gateway serves as but one of many moments in an experience requiring an extended period of time, a quiet marker in a personal, subtly focused exploration of the site. Secluded as it is from the other sculptures, *Bodark Arc* is discovered by the viewer rather than proclaimed by the sculptor, with the experience of the rugged, windswept prairie landscape as important as anything Puryear added to it.

If Puryear spent a great deal of time in the late 1970s and early 1980s pursuing outdoor projects, his studio work was dominated by a body of approximately forty sculptures that might be called "rings." These wall-mounted sculptures — the majority made of thin strips of wood which were laminated into roughly circular configurations — owe to *Circumbent*, the first laminated-wood piece, and to *Cedar Lodge*, the frame of which was constructed of rings of this type. In fact, it was while constructing *Cedar Lodge* at the Corcoran in 1977 that Puryear first conceived of the rings as potentially independent objects. Because of the fire, however, he was not able to begin working on them until after he had established himself in Chicago in 1978. Puryear introduced substantial variety into these sculptures despite their basically similar format. For example, only occasionally are the rings of a solid, circular shape; some, like *Big and Little Same*, 1981 (cat. no. 14), remain open forms with articulated endings. Rings such as *Untitled*, 1981-82 (cat. no. 16), bear faceted and beautifully painted surfaces. A few, for example, *Untitled*, 1978, and *Untitled*, 1982 (cats. nos. 10, 18), are not constructed at all, but consist rather of bent saplings.[60]

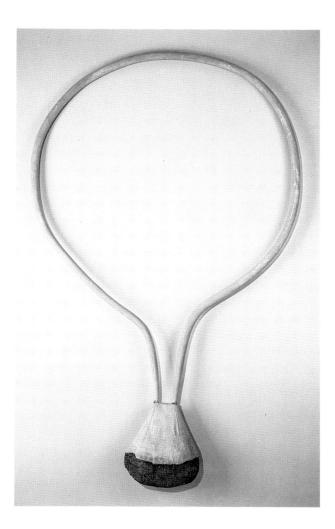

Fig. 29
Martin Puryear, *Untitled*, 1985
Painted pine, steel mesh, and Kozo paper
99 x 60 x 10 in.
Donald and Shirley Young, Seattle

While the rings possess an intimate, human scale and the circular form suggests a symbolic reference, these sculptures unquestionably reflect an impulse toward eloquent form and craftsmanship in Puryear's work. Perhaps the purest and most refined of these sculptures is *Cerulean*, 1982, in which the circle is unbroken and the surface is painted a quite luxuriant blue. And yet, after several exhibitions of the rings between 1978 and 1985, Puryear gradually came to tire of this purity. Puryear felt boxed in, for he recognized that the rings presented a limited format for a sculptor, and also that they implied an artifice and even a preciousness which the artist increasingly came to reject. Late rings such as *Endgame* and *Two into One*, both 1985 (cat. nos. 24, 28), show Puryear moving toward more physical forms. While *Two into One* is a more complex form, with two loops joined into a single sculpture, *Endgame* — aptly titled, for this would be the last ring — bears a muscular strength belying its carefully painted ends. Another work, *Untitled*, 1985 (fig. 29), clearly suggests a new direction: the scale is now much larger, and Puryear included a kind of sack made of steel mesh and Kozo paper, an element that suggests the downward pull of gravity. In the end Puryear determined to make his sculpture more vigorous, and toward that goal he forced himself to vary his materials. Frequently he began to employ wire and wire mesh, for example, despite his long-standing commitment to natural materials. Perhaps the most important relief sculpture made with wire is *Greed's Trophy*, 1984 (cat. no. 19), an enormous and open sculpture made without a hint of refined craft. A strong, aggressive, and quite direct work, the structure projects ominously out from the wall, suggesting nothing so much as a hunting trap, as implied by the title.

Fig. 30
Martin Puryear, *Vault*, 1984
Douglas fir, pine, hemlock, wire mesh,
and tar
99 x 97 x 48 in.
San Diego Museum of Contemporary Art,
San Diego, California

The same feeling of frustration with the artifice of the rings induced Puryear to concentrate quite consciously on sculpture in the round. This also involved new materials, particularly tar, which Puryear applied to wire mesh as a surface texture, with wood now serving simply as a structural element. The first piece of this sort was *Vault*, 1984 (fig. 30), in which the tar gives the sculpture a raw, tactile, and inelegant quality that was new to Puryear's sculpture. Another important work in which tar is employed is *Sanctum* (cat. no. 26). This sculpture is a dual-lobed, hutlike structure, the surface of which is composed of a patchwork quilt of mesh segments, collaged together and then tarred. Like *Cedar Lodge*, *Sanctum* is punctured by a hole at the top and the translucency of the surface and the fact that the structure does not rest evenly on the ground suggest a dynamic relationship between interior and exterior. The tar-covered mesh is at the heart of this perception: "I'm interested in mediating between a feeling of massiveness and fragility to reach a point of extreme vulnerability. Wire mesh allows for all of this. It can appear massive and opaque, but it is actually a thin veil."[61] In a sense, *Sanctum* can be considered a compact variation on a yurt; it is a small and lightweight shelter, and the tar lends the sculpture a roughness in keeping with its rugged outline.

Fig. 31
Martin Puryear, *Boy's Toys #7, #9, #12, #6,
and #13*, 1984
Mr. and Mrs. John Gabbert, Minneapolis
(#6, #7, #9, #12)
Roger and Neil Barrett, Winnetka, Illinois
(#13)

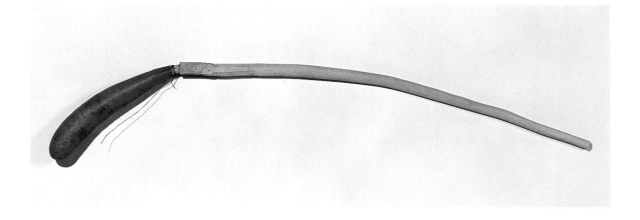

Fig. 32
Martin Puryear, *Boy's Toys # 1*, 1984
Yellow cedar, gourd, and wire
13½ × 72⅞ × 4½ in.
Mr. and Mrs. John Gabbert, Minneapolis

What begins to take hold in these sculptures is a shift away from the type of refinement that attention to craft can yield. Although Puryear has never abandoned craft, this dexterity is now expressed in a less self-conscious way, because materials such as wire mesh and tar are not easily subordinated to the hand. Yet while Puryear freed his work of excessive refinement, he did so without sacrificing the aura of the individual works and, in many ways, this has been a crucial element in the growth of his most recent sculpture. As Puryear would say in 1987, as if in reaction to the refinement he perceived in many of his rings, "I was never interested in making cool, distilled, pure objects. Although idea and form are ultimately paramount in my work, so too are chance, accident, and rawness."[62] These words introduce Puryear's recent work with great clarity. Beginning in the mid-1980s, with works such as *Sanctum* and *Greed's Trophy*, Puryear's sculpture has evolved with great vigor, diversity, and confidence. Beyond this, it is difficult to characterize the work at any given moment; Puryear has simultaneously pursued a number of themes, formal directions, and methods of construction, moving intrepidly and adventurously among these various possibilities.

One direction that Puryear has pursued rather continuously has been biomorphic form. There are subtle allusions to living beings in early pieces such as *Bask* and *Self* of the 1970s, but it was not until the mid-1980s that sculptures suggesting life appear with full force in Puryear's art. For example, in *Cask Cascade* and *Old Mole*, both 1985 (cat. nos. 23, 25), the forms seem to grow organically from the ground. The two works share an animallike torso below a slightly inclined neck and head. While the two sculptures are clearly mates, however, each is constructed differently: *Cask Cascade* is a faceted shell over a hollow interior core; *Old Mole* is wrapped randomly with lath strips while still retaining the overall contour and shape.

The anatomical suggestiveness of sculptures such as these could assume other forms and implications. In 1985 Puryear created a group of thirteen small sculptures which he called *Boy's Toys* (see figs. 31, 32). These works, many of them freestanding and measuring approximately forty to fifty inches in height, are constructed of various woods but also of gourds and copper tubing. Many possess solid, torsolike bottoms, yet these are now connected to phalliclike vertical elements. If several of the *Boy's Toys* playfully recall the male anatomy, others assume an objectlike character by virtue of their scale, materials, and paint surfaces, as well as by their titles. While the *Boy's Toys* would have rather immediate formal implications in Puryear's work, they are also intrinsically important because of their whimsy. Like the numerous small, playful sculptures made by Picasso in the 1930s, the *Boy's Toys* allow small-scale and humor to invade sculpture, often the most self-conscious and serious of artistic endeavors.

The same basic neck-and-body configuration in solid form characterizes several more recent works, much larger in scale, which Puryear made in 1987. These works — for example, *Empire's Lurch*, *Sharp and Flat*, and *Timber's Turn* (cat. nos. 29, 31, 32) — all allude to biomorphic form. Whereas several of the *Boy's Toys* reach straight upward in mock-phallic fashion, these later sculptures writhe and twist; they are bursting with arrested energy seeking release. Like *Sanctum*, *Timber's Turn* rests unevenly on the ground: head and body seem ready to rock into motion. We sense *Sharp and Flat* springing forward, the diagonal thrust of the neck seeming to urge the torso ahead; and *Empire's*

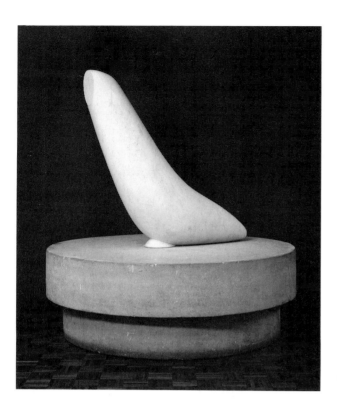

Fig. 33
Constantin Brancusi (Romanian, 1876–
1957), *The Seal (Miracle)*, 1924–32
White marble
42¾ x 44⅞ x 13 in.
The Solomon R. Guggenheim Museum,
New York

Lurch seems to rear back, as though an invisible rider had suddenly reined in and pulled the heavy dark green form to a sudden stop. The biomorphic aspect of these works is unmistakable and the theme continues in recent works such as *Lever #4* of 1989 (fig. 34), a wood sculpture painted gray. Although Puryear has described the piece formally as a "wedge tapered to a cone and then turned back on itself," the sculpture is now commonly referred to as "the seal," a characterization that is as much art historical as it is zoological; as Michael Brenson has aptly noted, *Lever #4* is reminiscent of Brancusi's *The Seal (Miracle)*, a great white marble sculpture of 1924-32 (fig. 33).[63]

If many of Puryear's recent sculptures suggest living forms, they possess other organic characteristics as well. Most of these sculptures were clearly and decisively constructed in milled woods such as pine, cedar, mahogany, and Douglas fir. The surfaces are generally solid, suggesting a clear and unbroken chain of development from conception to completion. All have an organic rightness about them, a surety of mind and hand that lends each an unmistakable formal authority.[64]

Another group of recent works suggests a different impulse altogether. In contrast to the organic and even biomorphic character of the foregoing works, Puryear has also made sculptures that suggest objects and artifacts. These works possess an allusiveness that is cultural rather than natural; as Puryear notes, they suggest "objects that are the product of a conscious mind."[65] Among recent works in this vein are two dating to 1987. *Untitled* (cat. no. 34), of tar-over-mesh-over-wood construction, contrasts two parts: a floor-based, nearly oval element which rests solidly on the ground, and a looping upper element. The contrast is between linearity and lightness above and solidity and weight below and, simultaneously, between negative and positive, void and solid, and open and closed. The sculpture suggests an implement as the upper element can be read as a fantastically large handle, meant to lift and move the sculpture. Another work in this vein is *Noblesse O.*, also of 1987 (cat. no. 30). The objectlike nature of this tapering cone derives from the treatment of the surface, which Puryear painted with aluminum paint, an aspect that places the sculpture at a further remove from the natural world of wood, and thereby suggestive of objects rather than beings.

More recently, Puryear has produced sculptures that fuse references to objects and living forms, creating an abstraction of renewed vigor. In some cases this is the result of the sculptor's willingness to change a sculpture, sometimes dramatically, even after it has been exhibited. Recognizing the value of seeing a new work, particularly a large work, outside the studio before pronouncing it complete, on several occasions Puryear has looked on the initial exhibition of a work as a test of its form. An example of this was an enormous, initially untitled work (fig. 35), a black, egg-shaped structure composed of a patchwork translucent tar-over-mesh surface with one side bearing rough wood planking punctured by a square hole. Puryear considered this bulbous black form to be the principal element, and he subsequently conceived of a series of long elements that might be attached to it on different occasions. The first — and ultimately the only one — proved to be a thirty-foot-long train of open-weave rattan, through which the artist meant to suggest a beached vessel. Yet when Puryear exhibited the piece at the Donald Young Gallery in Chicago in 1987, he became dissatisfied with this latter element as unnecessary and perhaps too close to tribal forms. He decided to retain only the original black element, jettisoning the rattan or any other possible additive ele-

Fig. 34
Martin Puryear, *Lever #4*, 1989
Painted red cedar
96 x 81 x 43 in.
Mr. and Mrs. Harry W. Anderson, Atherton,
California

ments and choosing instead to emphasize the abrupt end which he now preferred. Since that time Puryear has employed various objects as shims to keep the rounded mesh and tar form from shifting, and he has subsequently exhibited the sculpture under the title *Maroon* (cat. no. 35).[66]

Interestingly, when Puryear showed the original work at the Donald Young Gallery in 1987, he contrasted it with two other works, both possessing similar truncated intersections, both at a much reduced scale. One was an earlier work, *Untitled*, 1982 (cat. no. 18), a ring in which Puryear had abruptly conjoined a bent sapling and an egg-shaped knob. The other was a new work, *To Transcend*, 1987 (cat. no. 33). Here approximately the same roughly oval form is again reduced dramatically in scale and now tipped on end so that it functions as a base element. In all three works — the original version of *Maroon*, the untitled ring, and *To Transcend* — Puryear concentrated on the resolution of tenuous relationships, contrasting the egg-shaped form with a variety of extensions with extreme shifts in scale.

By 1988 Puryear was juggling matters of form and scale, and changing sculptures in dramatic fashion, with great aplomb. This is the case with *Lever #1*, 1988-89 (cat. no. 38), an emphatically upright sculpture which is among Puryear's most imposing works. The sculpture consists of two parts: an open vessel which is tall and exceedingly narrow, and a dramatically arched top member, the shape of which echoes the opening below and seems poised to slam down upon it. Interpretations of this piece vary widely, from allusions to sexual union to a coffin, and from an oversize Japanese headdress to a deep-hulled boat.[67] Puryear has himself suggested the theme of mortality, and one can clearly conceive of the sculpture as an open coffin awaiting burial. The variety of chords that the sculpture strikes serves to activate the piece, as does the surface, which is alive with the remnants of glue, staples, and the entire process of working.

As Puryear worked on the sculpture, gluing and stapling thin strips of red cedar to the base, he decided to reduce the height of the hollow trough — which was originally above eye level and thus too high for most people to look into. In order to reduce the height, Puryear cut away an approximately two-foot-high horizontal band from the top of the base. He promptly mounted this element on the wall of his studio where it took the form of a variation on one of the earlier rings, now in the shape of a very long and deep slit. This untitled work (fig. 36) was made early in 1988, at precisely the time Puryear was preparing a group of similar works for exhibition. One of the most accomplished of these new wall-mounted sculptures is *The Cut*, 1988 (cat. no. 36), which possesses similarly long and narrow dimensions but now with the addition of a solid back. This element is crucial, because it transforms the sculpture from a purely abstract form to one that resembles a useful object. Yet, like Joseph Beuys's *Jason II*, 1962 (fig. 37), a bathtub mounted on the wall, or like the Shaker furniture that Puryear so admires, once an object is hung on a wall, its functional implications may be neutralized and the form read as abstract.[68]

This flexible process, in which a piece may change dramatically even after it has been exhibited, and in which the castoff elements of one piece may reappear in a different form and context, also occurred in 1988 with another large originally untitled piece. As originally conceived, this work consisted of two elements: an open, horizontal rattan frame with a bell-shaped end, and a slightly curved, upright member topped by a solid, cone-shaped cap. Puryear conceived of this work as a reference to polygamy with the magisterial vertical element reigning over a series of recumbent horizontals. Yet, when he saw the sculpture exhibited in 1988 at the St. Louis Art Museum, Puryear decided to alter the vertical, transforming it into a sweeping horizontal curve, and concluding that this rather languorous element better resolved the sculpture without sacrificing the theme.[69] Puryear titled the final version of this work *Lever #2* (cat. no. 39) and, along with its predecessor, *Lever #1*, it stands as one of Puryear's finest and most ambitious works to date.

The body of work that Puryear completed between 1987 and 1990 is remarkable for both its quality and its range. The confidence that the sculptor has exhibited here is unmistakable, as he has demonstrated a willingness and an ability to test and transform works in dramatic and unexpected ways, both in the studio and in public. This is apparent in the sculptures that were resolved following exhibition, and in the way in which fragments that were rejected in one work could provide the impetus for new sculptures. Beyond this, the recent sculptures suggest a seemingly limitless array of visual references. Whether one perceives the sculptures as biomorphic or objective, every viewer seems to have a response and a plausible and often unexpected reading. And yet, Puryear resolutely considers himself — and he clearly is — an abstract sculptor. He travels great lengths to resolve his sculptures from a purely formal standpoint, but also to ensure that no single, superficial reading of a work may prevail. Beyond this, he is apt to reject sculptures that seem to yield only one reading. One senses the artist pushing himself, seeking answers that will make the work undeniably original

Fig. 36
Martin Puryear, *Untitled*, 1988
Red cedar and pine
9 ft. 5 in. × 22 in. × 17 in.
Mr. and Mrs. Thomas H. Dittmer, Lake Forest, Illinois

49

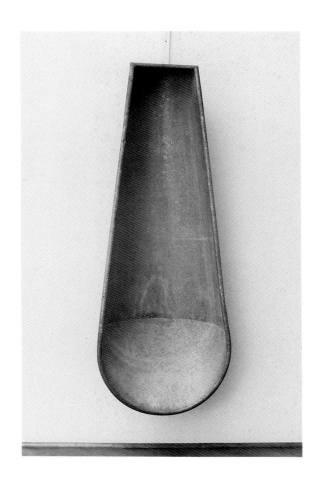

Fig. 37
Joseph Beuys (German, 1921–1986),
Jason II, 1962
Wood, paint, and iron
94½ x 26⅝ x 17⅜ in.
Bernd and Verena Klüser, Munich

and apart from anything one has seen in art, life, or nature. There is a reassertion of the power of abstract art implied here, as Puryear has found that abstraction is capable of encompassing a very broad range of working methods and visual effects. His is an abstraction that is accessible without being obvious.

This quality was never more evident than at the 1989 São Paulo Bienal. Selected as the official United States representative, Puryear exhibited a group of eight works representing several moments in his career, but emphasizing recent works from the *Lever* series (see figs. 38, 39). This installation, for which Puryear won the grand prize, was received with great surprise and enthusiasm by the mostly South American critics and visitors. Unquestionably, most were unfamiliar with Puryear's work, and its appeal was great on several levels. First was certainly the manner in which Puryear works with wood, a material more commonly employed by South American sculptors than by North Americans. More interesting, however, was the surprise that the work engendered in terms of the originality and universality of its form. Although this principally non-European/non-North American audience had never before seen work like this, Puryear's sculpture seemed to communicate both materially, but also, perhaps more importantly, on the basis of its physical presence and the breadth of its cross-cultural references. As Michael Brenson has aptly noted, "Puryear has the ability to make sculpture that is known by the body before it is articulated by the mind."[70]

The implications of this observation reveal much about Puryear's work. Puryear's appeal to emotional and physical levels of experience, and not just to a cognitive response, extends the implications of his sculpture well beyond the immediacy of ambition and reach of much contemporary art. In this and several other ways, Puryear reinvigorates a modern tradition that contemporary sculptors often reject. In contrast to the conceptual activity of many artists, Puryear reasserts the working process and the ethical value of the artist making objects in the studio. Here Puryear's modernism is akin to that of sculptors ranging from Richard Serra to the Englishman Richard Deacon: artists committed to the physical activity traditionally associated with making sculpture. Puryear's modernism is characterized by an obsessive need to work, and the structural integrity and lively surfaces of his sculpture testify to this physical involvement. Beyond this, Puryear's modernism includes the craft tradition that was such an important aspect of American creative culture in the 1960s. For Puryear, originality remains a crucial impetus, not in the sense of striving for a signature style, but rather as a governing idea: the artist moving ever-forward, avoiding repetition and often surprising himself and his public by the unexpected possibilities his work might yield. Just as Puryear became dissatisfied with the limitations of craft, and even with his own work at times, so he has been willing to reconstitute his sculptures when they have not lived well in the world. Here Puryear's work contrasts with much recent American sculpture that has suffered in the strait-jacket of formalism. Rather than accepting self-imposed limits necessitated by an obsession with form, Puryear has strived to make his work one of possibilities and abundance. That is, while many sculptors working in the Minimalist tradition have excluded associative reference from modern sculpture, Puryear has reasserted the inclusiveness of modernism, allowing and even encouraging allusion and metaphor to enrich and complicate his work.

Figs. 38, 39
Installation of Martin Puryear sculpture at
the "20th International São Paulo Bienal,"
1989

What Puryear values in modernism is originality and change, aspects that he considers life-affirming and regenerative. In this sense Puryear shares much with Europeans such as Beuys, Long, Merz, and the Greek-born Jannis Kounellis, artists with little formal similarity, but with expansive notions of art and its possibilities and with extended cultural memories. Although one would not describe him as uninterested in style — in contrast to the English sculptor Tony Cragg who peripatetically explores new materials and forms — Puryear has become adept at shifting directions rather suddenly in order to explore a new avenue for his work. This is identifiable at several moments in Puryear's career, and most recently in a work such as *Thicket*, 1990 (cat. no. 40). If we had come to expect an emphasis on skin in the mesh-and-tar sculptures such as *Sanctum* of the mid-1980s, *Thicket* is all skeleton, thereby proclaiming the artist's commitment to change as well as a refusal to be cornered stylistically. In short, while Puryear retains the strong commitment to form that is his legacy from Minimalism and the American modern tradition, he combines this with an anthropological openness, for his is a sensibility enriched by experience in Africa, Europe, and Asia.

Puryear understands the disillusion that has bred a current wave of critical attitudes toward modern art and contemporary culture, yet he does not consider an often nostalgic reinterpretation of past styles, nor a cynical analysis of contemporary cultural forms, to be viable approaches to making art. Although Puryear is himself critical of much in contemporary society, he believes that this only underscores the need for an art that is original and undogmatic. That is, while Puryear recognizes the postmodernist loss of faith, this only enlarges his faith in himself and his art as a way of transcending traditions of all sorts. Rather than pessimism, Puryear exudes an enthusiasm for life, experience, and the next sculpture in the studio. In conversation, he likens his belief in art to that of Jof, the simple juggler in the Swedish director Ingmar Bergman's film *The Seventh Seal*. While the knight struggles valiantly to confound death and the devil in a futile game of chess, Jof remains possessed of thoughts and visions, of an innocent sense of self, and of a future beyond.

NOTES

1. Soetsu Yanagi, "The Buddhist Idea of Beauty," in *The Unknown Craftsman* (Tokyo and New York: Kodansha International, 1972), pp. 129–30.

2. Yanagi, "The Way of Craftsmanship," in *The Unknown Craftsman* (note 1), p. 200.

3. Puryear, in conversation with the author, March 9, 1990.

4. Puryear, in conversation with the author, August 10, 1990.

5. Puryear, in conversation with the author, December 14, 1990.

6. Ibid.

7. Sonneman, from a letter to the author dated July 1, 1990. I am very grateful to Nell Sonneman for her consideration and assistance.

8. Ibid.

9. Puryear, in Amherst, Massachusetts, University Gallery, University of Massachusetts, *Martin Puryear*, exhibition catalogue by Hugh M. Davies and Helaine Posner (Amherst, 1984), p. 32.

10. Puryear (note 3).

11. Puryear (note 5).

12. Puryear, in Mary Swift and Clarissa Wittenberg, "An Interview with Martin Puryear," *The Washington Review* 4, 3 (October/November 1978), p. 33.

13. Puryear, in Amherst, Massachusetts (note 9), p. 31.

14. Ibid.

15. Puryear (note 3).

16. Krenov, in conversation with the author, August 21, 1989. Krenov is the author of four books: *A Cabinetmaker's Notebook* (New York: Prentice-Hall, Inc., 1976); *The Fine Art of Cabinetmaking* (New York: Prentice-Hall Press, 1977); *The Impractical Cabinetmaker* (New York: Prentice Hall Press, 1979); and *James Krenov: Worker in Wood* (New York: Van Nostrand Reinhold Company, 1981).

17. Puryear (note 3).

18. Puryear, in Amherst, Massachusetts (note 9), p. 30.

19. Puryear (note 5).

20. Puryear, in Amherst, Massachusetts (note 9), p. 32.

21. Puryear (note 5).

22. Ibid.

23. See, for example, the summer 1967 issue of *Artforum*, an issue devoted entirely to avant-garde sculpture and including seminal articles by Sol LeWitt and Robert Morris, among others.

24. The crucial series of articles by Robert Morris are "Notes on Sculpture," *Artforum* 4 (February 1966), pp. 42–44; "Notes on Sculpture, Part 2," *Artforum* 5 (October 1966), pp. 20–23; "Notes on Sculpture, Part 3," *Artforum* 5 (Summer 1967), pp. 24–29; and "Anti-Form," *Artforum* 6 (April 1968), pp. 33–35. For LeWitt, see "Paragraphs on Conceptual Art," *Artforum* 5 (Summer 1967), pp. 79–83.

25. Post-Minimalism is documented in an outstanding new exhibition catalogue: New York, Whitney Museum of American Art, *The New Sculpture 1965–75: Between Geometry and Gesture*, exhibition catalogue by Richard Armstrong and Richard Marshall (New York, 1990).

26. Puryear (note 5).

27. Puryear (note 3).

28. Puryear (note 5).

29. Paul Richard, "Martin Puryear at Henri 2," *The Washington Post*, 1973. The specific date of this article, published on the occasion of Puryear's second exhibition at the Henri Gallery in 1973, cannot be determined.

30. David Bourdon, "Martin Puryear at Henri 2," *Art in America* 62, 1 (January/February 1974), p. 110.

31. Puryear (note 5).

32. Ibid.

33. Puryear (note 4).

34. Ibid.

35. Puryear (note 5).

36. Puryear, in Paul Richard, "The Sculpture of Longing," *The Washington Post*, March 25, 1988, p. D2.

37. Puryear, in Amherst, Massachusetts (note 9), p. 23.

38. *Where the Heart Is (Sleeping Mews)* has been exhibited at the and/or gallery, Seattle, 1981; in "Martin Puryear: Public and Personal," Chicago Public Library Cultural Center, 1987; and in "Connections: Martin Puryear," Museum of Fine Arts, Boston, 1990. I am grateful to Ramona Austin for her comments on Puryear's chair.

39. Puryear, in Amherst, Massachusetts (note 9), p. 30.

40. Robert Storr, "Martin Puryear: The Hand's Proportion," in Jamaica, New York, Jamaica Arts Center, *Martin Puryear,* 20th International São Paulo Bienal 1989, exhibition catalogue by Kellie Jones (Jamaica, 1989), p. 25. This article is reprinted here in a slightly revised and updated form.

41. Puryear, in conversation with the author, March 17, 1990. See also Matthew A. Henson, *A Negro Explorer at the North Pole* (New York: Arno Press and The New York Times, 1969); and Wally Herbert, *The Noose of Laurels: Robert E. Peary and the Race to the North Pole* (New York: Atheneum, 1989).

42. See *Encyclopedia Brittanica*, 15th edition, 1988, pp. 34–35.

43. Puryear, in Richard (note 36), p. D2.

44. Puryear, in Amherst, Massachusetts (note 9), p. 25.

45. Puryear (note 5).

46. Puryear, in Amherst, Massachusetts (note 9), p. 30.

47. Puryear, in Eileen Thalenberg, "Site Work: Some Sculpture at Artpark 1977," *Artscanada* 216/217 (October/November 1977), p. 18. For an overview of Puryear's outdoor works, see Patricia Fuller, "Martin Puryear: Public Places, Personal Vision," in Chicago, Chicago Public

Library Cultural Center, *Martin Puryear: Public and Personal*, exhibition catalogue by Deven K. Golden (Chicago, 1987), pp. 30–48.

48. Puryear's comments were recorded in 1977 in a videotape interview now in the collection of the Video Data Bank of The School of The Art Institute of Chicago. I am grateful to Eunice Fitzgibbons for her transcription.

49. See Seattle, Washington, National Oceanic and Atmospheric Administration, Western Regional Center, *Five Artists at NOAA: A Casebook on Art in Public Places,* essay by Patricia Fuller (Seattle: The Real Comet Press, 1985).

50. Ibid., pp. 14, 20.

51. Puryear's design was commissioned by the Fairmount Park Art Association for Cliveden Park in Philadelphia. See Grace Glueck, "Serving the Environment," *The New York Times*, June 27, 1982, pp. H25– 26; and Fuller (note 47), p. 38. For the *njâllâ*, see Roberto Bosi, *The Lapps*, trans. James Cadell (1960; rpt. Westport, Connecticut: Greenwood Press, 1976), pp. 87, 212, fig. 21. For the *honden*, see Yasutada Watanabe, *Shinto Art: Ise and Izumo Shrines*, trans. Robert Ricketts (New York: Weatherhill/Heibonsha, 1974). I am grateful to James Ulak for his suggestions concerning the *honden*.

52. Puryear, in Amherst, Massachusetts (note 9), p. 31.

53. Serra, in Douglas Crimp, "Richard Serra's Urban Sculpture: An Interview," in Yonkers, New York, The Hudson River Museum, *Richard Serra: Interviews, Etc., 1970–1980* (Yonkers, 1980), p. 170.

54. Ibid., p. 168.

55. Long, in New York, The Solomon R. Guggenheim Museum, *Richard Long*, exhibition catalogue by R. H. Fuchs (New York, 1986), p. 236.

56. For outstanding photographs of Brancusi's work at Tirgu Jiu, see Eric Shanes, *Constantin Brancusi* (New York: Abbeville Press, 1989), pp. 82–97.

57. University Park, Illinois, Governors State University, *The Nathan Manilow Sculpture Park*, essay by Peter Schjeldahl (University Park, 1987), pp. 21–27.

58. Puryear, in Amherst, Massachusetts (note 9), p. 28.

59. Ibid., p. 32.

60. To a great extent, critical commentary on the rings has been conditioned by the context in which they have been shown. Perhaps the most striking example of this phenomenon occurred when Puryear exhibited a series of rings in "Afro-American Abstraction," a much-discussed group exhibition that toured the United States in 1980–82. The respected *New York Times* critic John Russell described these works as "sculpture, quite rightly, but they could moonlight as chokers for a giantess: we recognize at once the ennobling assurance with which Africans used to endow objects of daily use" (Russell, "Abstractions from Afro-America," *The New York Times*, March 14, 1980, sec. 3, p. 19). Similarly, Robert Hughes, reviewing the same exhibition, described one of Puryear's rings as "a minimal serpent with a knob for a head: this handsome and assured object is like a blowup of a tribal bracelet, but with more sculptural presence" (Hughes, "Going Back to Africa— as Visitors," *Time* 115, 13 [March 31, 1980], p. 72).

61. Puryear, in New York, Whitney Museum of American Art at Equitable Center, *Enclosing the Void: Eight Contemporary Sculptors*, exhibition catalogue by Susan Lubowsky (New York, 1988), p. 5.

62. Puryear, in Pittsburgh, Carnegie Mellon University, Hewlett Art Gallery, *Martin Puryear: Sculpture and Works on Paper*, exhibition brochure by Elaine King (Pittsburgh, 1987), n.pag.

63. Michael Brenson, "A Sculptor's Struggle to Fuse Culture and Art," *The New York Times*, October 29, 1989, p. H39.

64. Puryear has told me that, appearances to the contrary, he had great difficulty resolving the neck element in *Empire's Lurch*, attempting several solutions before arriving at the current form. Puryear, in conversation with the author, October 17, 1990.

65. Ibid.

66. Puryear (note 5).

67. Brenson (note 63), p. 39.

68. Puryear has noted his admiration for Beuys: "Beuys was not stylistically concerned and he was his own kind, with his own sense of direction and statement" (Puryear, in Pittsburgh [note 62]). These reliefs were exhibited at the McIntosh-Drysdale Gallery in Washington, D.C., in 1988. My colleague Charles Stuckey has reminded me that the act of mounting independent sculptures on the wall may well have been initiated by Picasso, with his *Guitar* of 1912.

69. Puryear (note 64).

70. Michael Brenson, "Maverick Sculptor Makes Good," *The New York Times*, November 1, 1987, sec. 5, p. 90.

PLATES

RAWHIDE CONE, 1974 (second version, 1980; original destroyed in 1977) (cat. no. 1)
Rawhide, 51 x 63 x 32 in.
Collection of the artist

SOME TALES, 1975–77 (cat. no. 2) (see pp. 58–59)
Ash and yellow pine, 30 ft. long (approximately)
Panza di Biumo Collection, Milan

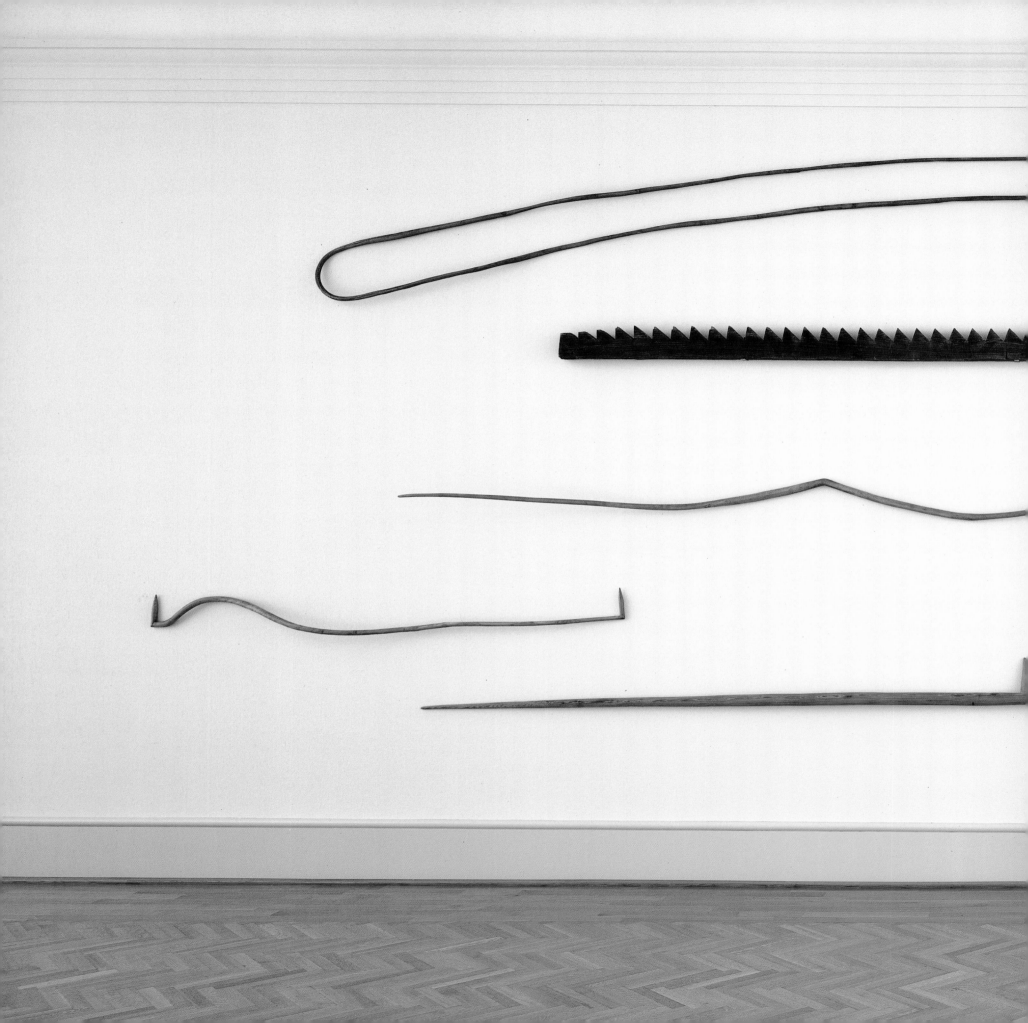

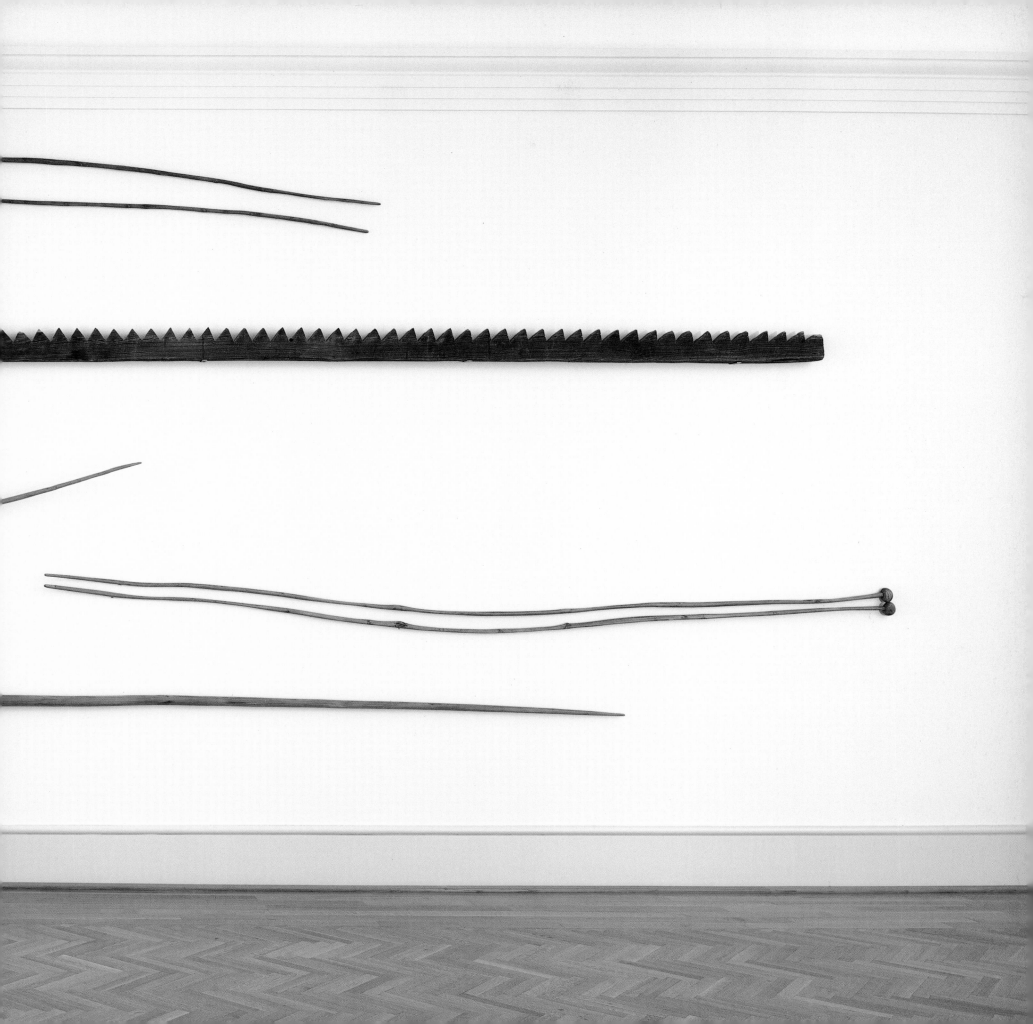

BASK, 1976 (cat. no. 3)
Staved dyed pine, 12 in. × 12 ft. 2¾ in. × 24 in.
Solomon R. Guggenheim Museum, New York,
Exxon Corporation Purchase Award

CIRCUMBENT, 1976 (cat. no. 4)
Ash, 64 in. × 9 ft. 11¾ in. × 21 in.
Collection of the artist

STRIPLING, 1976 (cat. no. 5)
Ash, 85 × 10 in.
Truland Systems Corporation, Arlington, Virginia

BELIEVER, 1977–82 (cat. no. 6)
Poplar and pine, 23¼ × 23⅜ × 17⅜ in.
Collection of the artist

SELF, 1978 (cat. no. 7)
Painted cedar and mahogany, 69 x 48 x 25 in.
Joslyn Art Museum, Omaha, Nebraska, Purchase in memory of Elinor Ashton

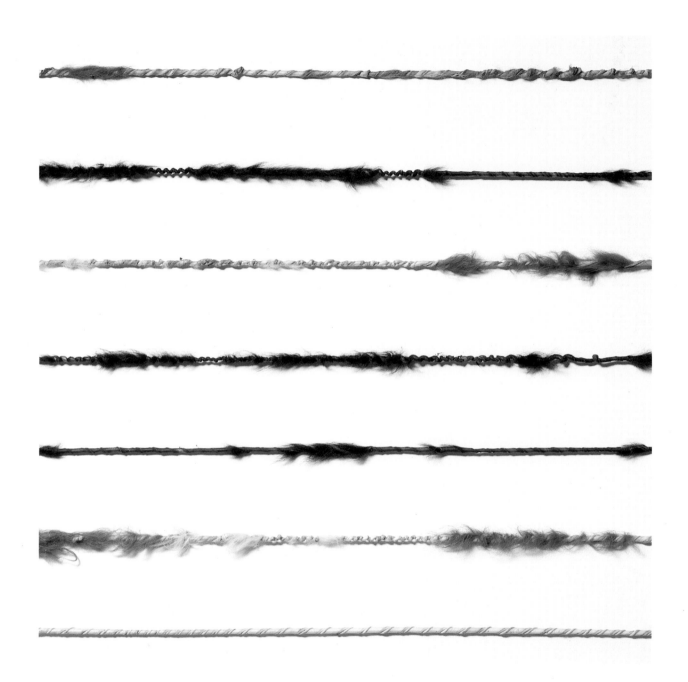

SOME LINES FOR JIM BECKWOURTH, 1978 (cat. no. 8)
Twisted rawhide, 23 ft. long (approximately)
Collection of the artist

UNTITLED, 1978 (cat. no. 9)
African blackwood and vine, 15⅞ in. long
Truland Systems Corporation, Arlington, Virginia

UNTITLED, 1978 (cat. no. 10)
Hickory and Alaskan yellow cedar, 60 x 78 x 1 in.
Nancy and Douglas Drysdale, Washington, D.C.

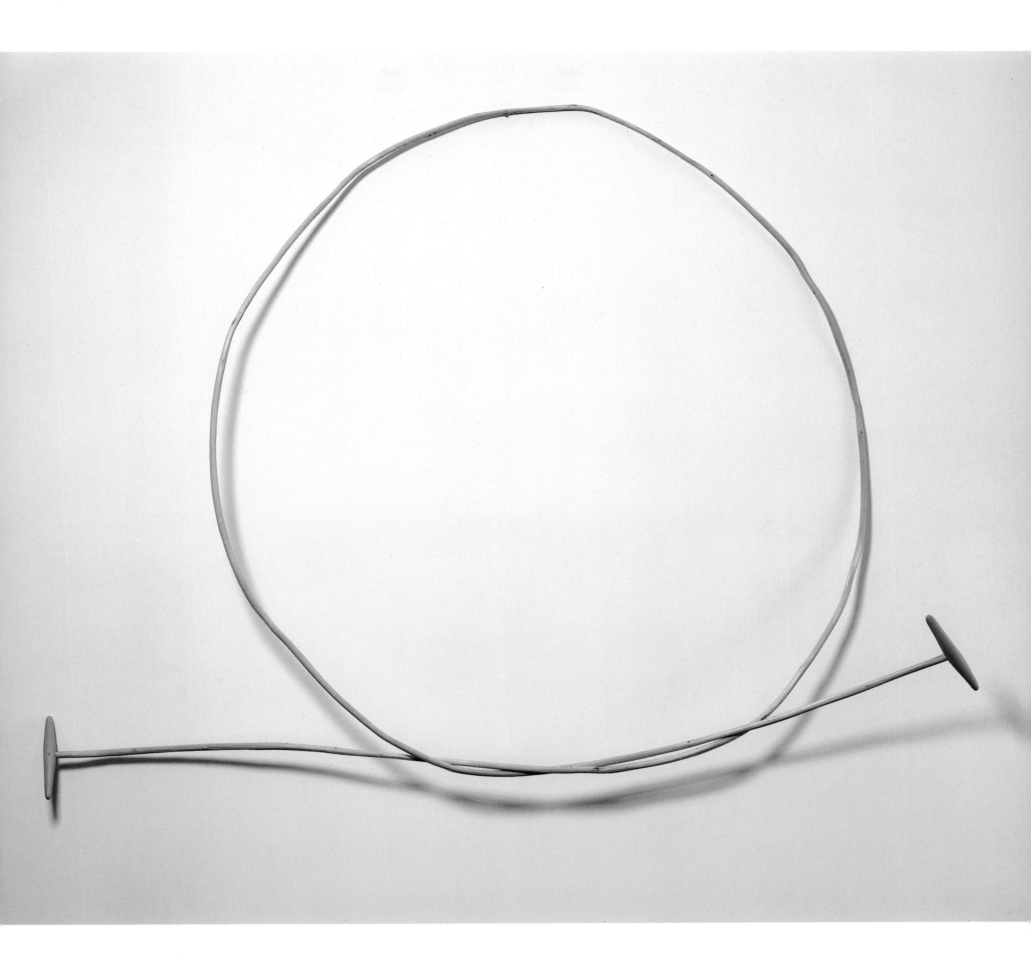

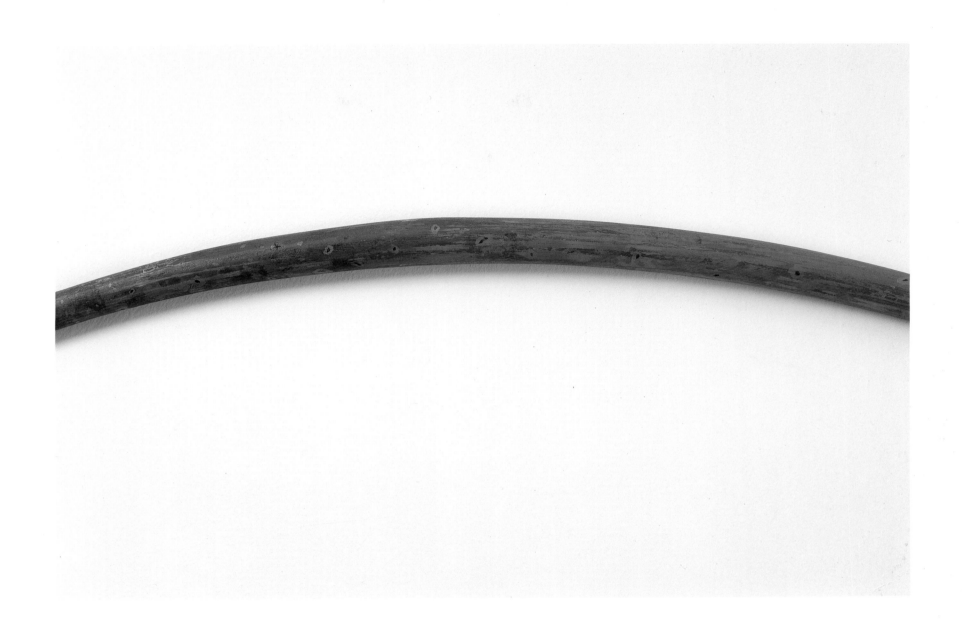

PRIMAVERA, 1979 (cat. no. 11)
Painted pine and maple, 64¾ × 64 × 2 in.
Nancy A. Drysdale, Washington, D.C.

BOWER, 1980 (cat. no. 12)
Pine and Sitka spruce, 64 × 94¾ × 26⅝ in.
The Oliver-Hoffmann Collection, Chicago

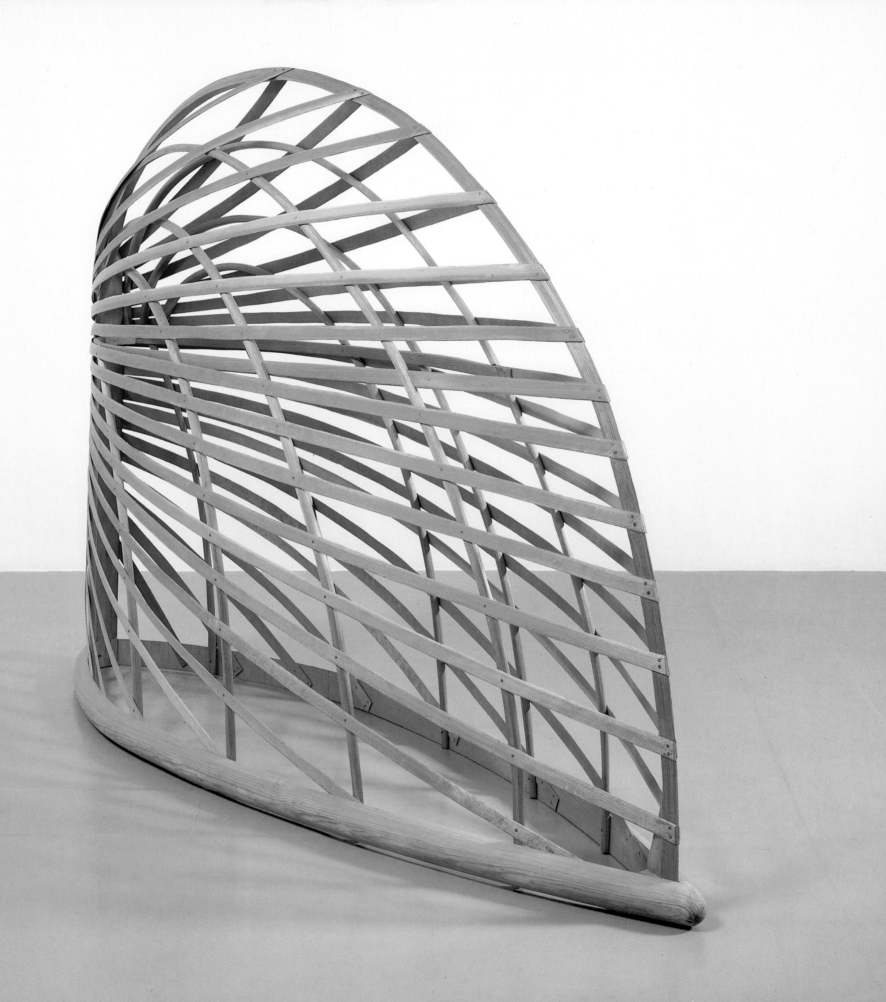

FOR BECKWOURTH, 1980 (cat. no. 13)
Earth, pitch pine, and oak, 40 × 34 × 34 in.
Collection of the artist

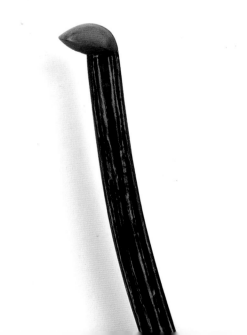

BIG AND LITTLE SAME, 1981 (cat. no. 14)
Ponderosa pine, painted pine, and unpainted pear wood, 61 × 62 × 2¾ in.
Councilman Joel Wachs, Los Angeles

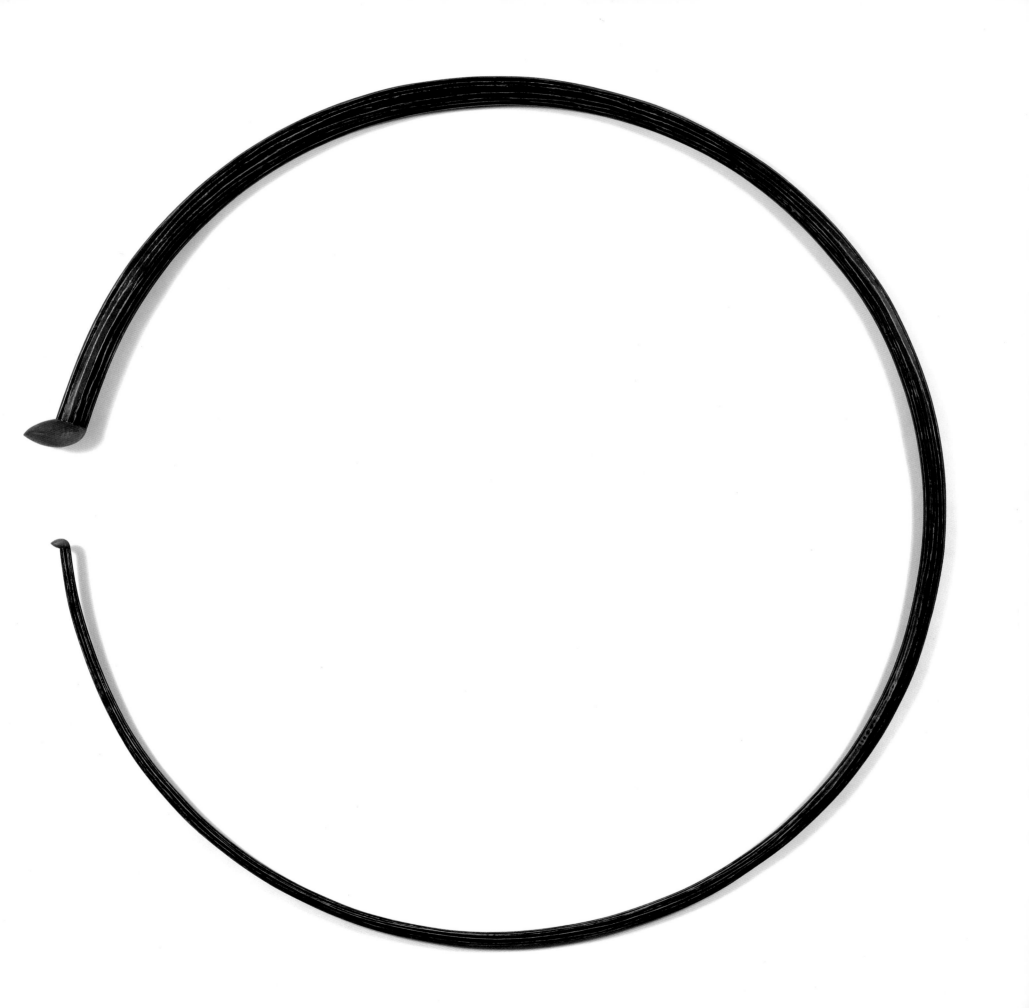

DREAM OF PAIRING, 1981 (cat. no. 15)
Painted pine, 51½ x 54½ x 2 in.
Alice Kleberg Reynolds, Artemis Investments, San Antonio, Texas

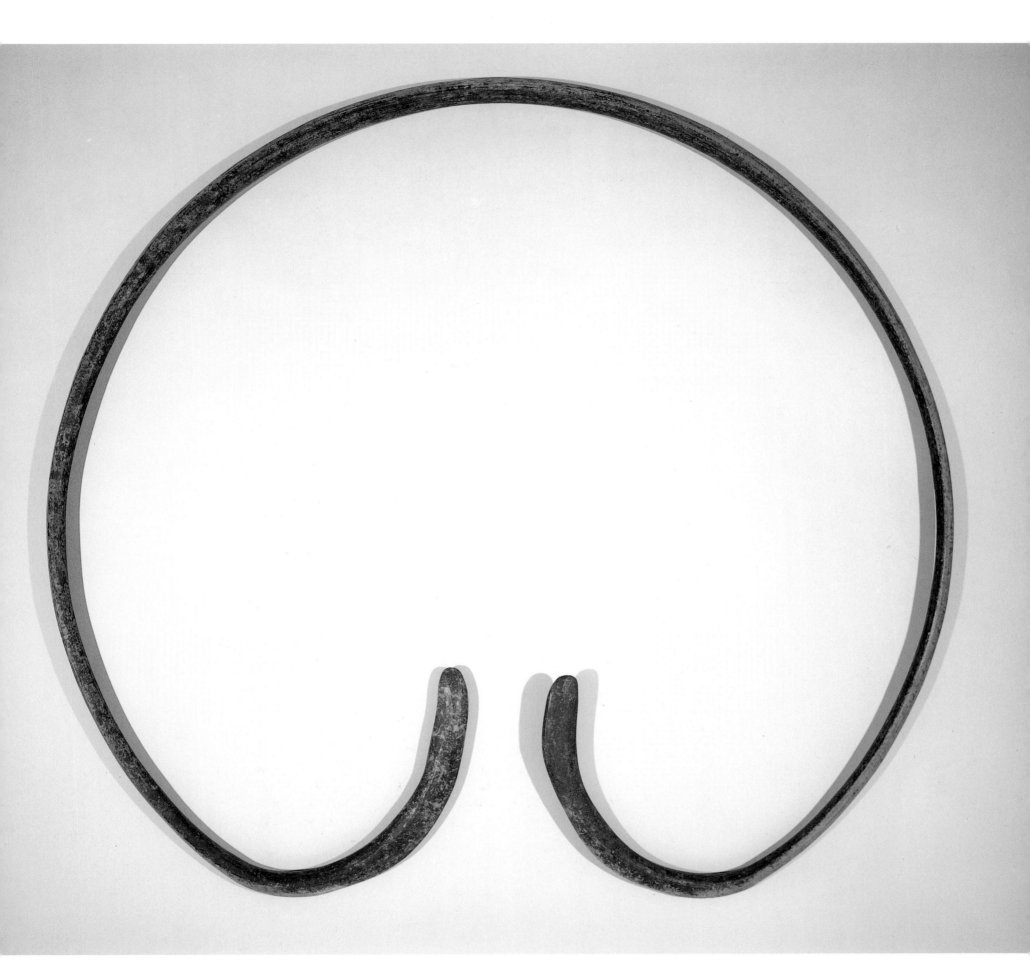

UNTITLED, 1981 –82 (cat. no. 16)
Painted ponderosa pine, 58 in. diameter x 9⅜ in.
Murray Bring, New York

SANCTUARY, 1982 (cat. no. 17)
Pine, maple, and cherry, 10 ft. 6 in. × 24 in. × 18 in.
The Art Institute of Chicago, Mr. and Mrs. Frank G. Logan Prize Fund, 1982.1473

UNTITLED, 1982 (cat. no. 18)
Maple sapling, pear wood, and yellow cedar, 59 x 66 x 5 in.
Judith and Edward Neisser, Chicago

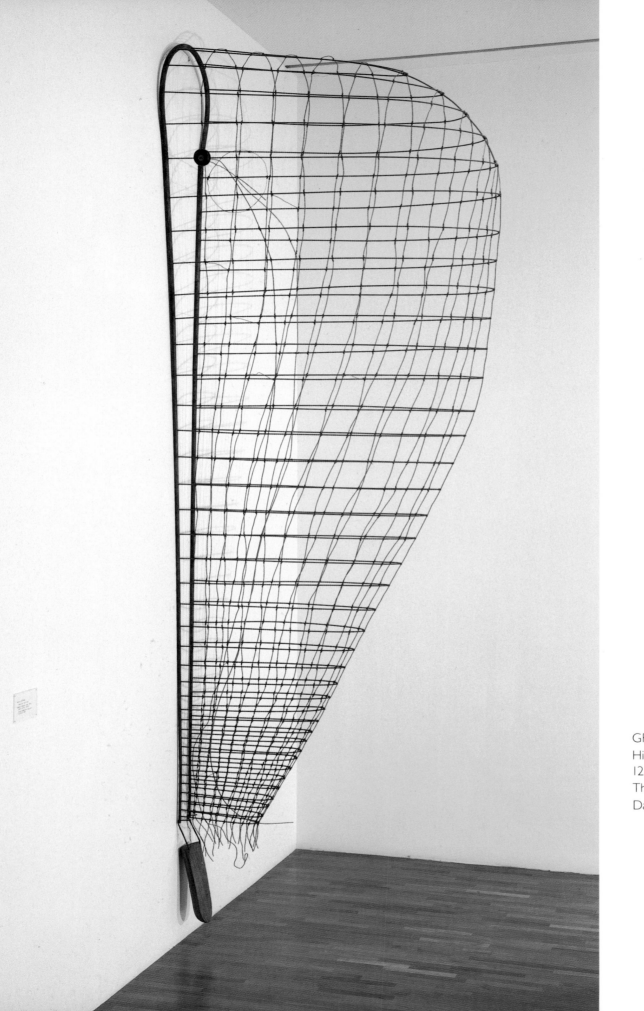

GREED'S TROPHY, 1984 (cat. no. 19)
Hickory, ebony, rattan, steel, and wire,
12 ft. 9 in. x 20 in. x 55 in.
The Museum of Modern Art, New York,
David Rockefeller Fund and Purchase

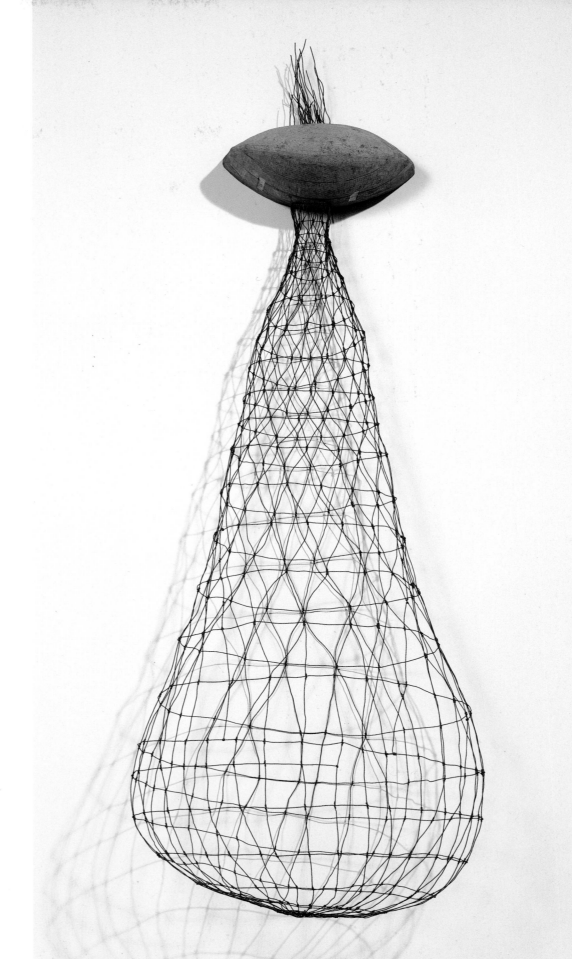

KEEPER, 1984 (cat. no. 20)
Pine and steel wire, 8 ft. 4 in. × 34 in. × 38 in.
Alan and Wendy Hart, Topanga, California

LURK, 1984 (cat. no. 21)
Painted pine, 21¾ x 61¼ x 7¼ in.
Collection of Margo Leavin, Los Angeles

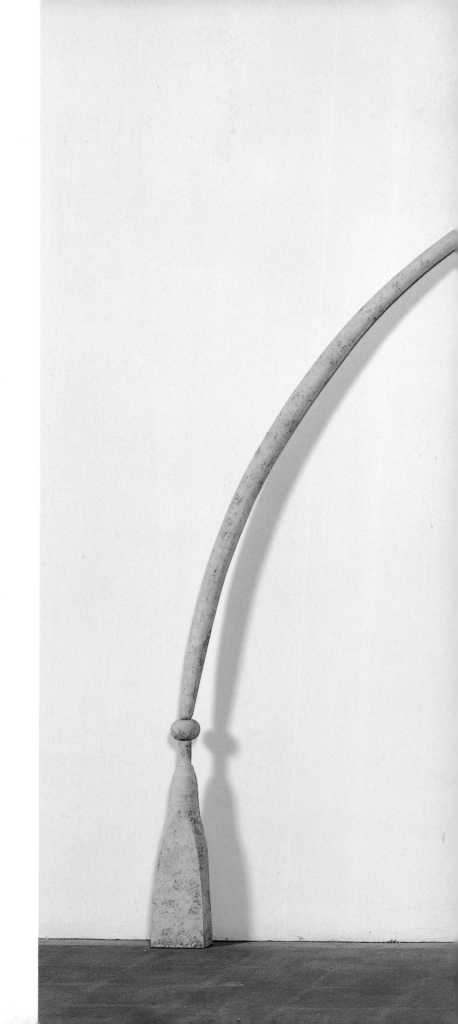

NIGHT AND DAY, 1984 (cat. no. 22)
Painted pine and wire, 75 in. x 10 ft. x 6 in.
The Patsy N. and Raymond D. Nasher Collection, Dallas

CASK CASCADE, 1985 (cat. no. 23)
Painted red cedar, 61¾ x 59½ x 30¼ in.
John and Mary Pappajohn, Des Moines, Iowa

ENDGAME, 1985 (cat. no. 24)
Painted pine, 65 × 66 × 5 in.
REFCO Group, Ltd., Chicago

OLD MOLE, 1985 (cat. no. 25)
Red cedar, 61 x 61 x 32 in.
Philadelphia Museum of Art: Purchased: The Samuel S. White, 3rd, and
Vera White Collection (by exchange) and Gift of Mr. and Mrs. C. G. Chaplin
(by exchange) and funds contributed by Marion Stroud Swingle, and funds
contributed by friends and family in memory of Mrs. H. Gates Lloyd

SANCTUM, 1985 (cat. no. 26)
Pine, wire mesh, and tar, 76 in. × 9 ft. 1 in. × 87 in.
Whitney Museum of American Art, New York,
Purchase, with funds from the Painting and Sculpture Committee, 85.72

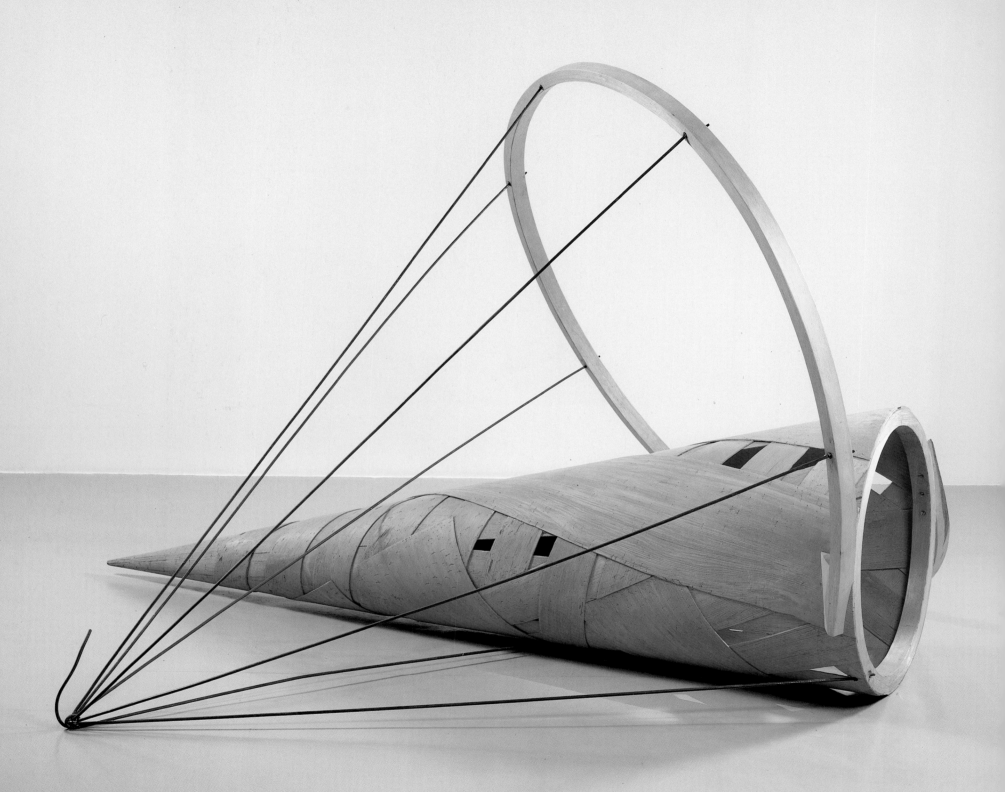

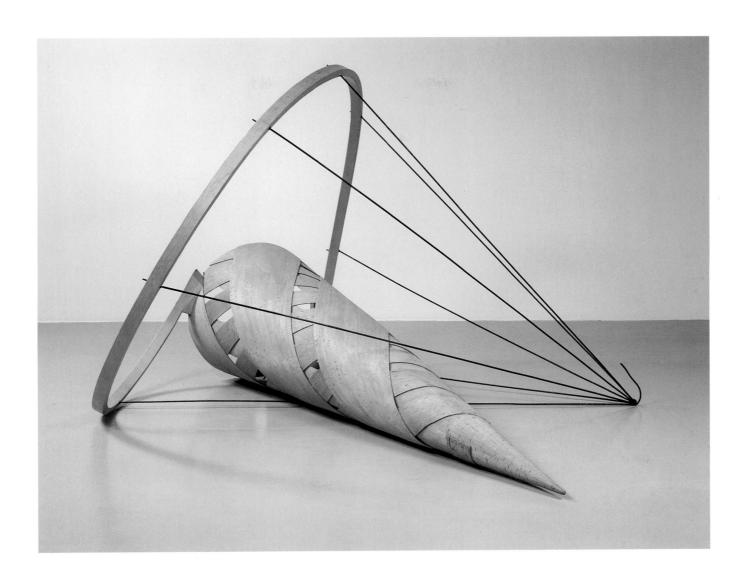

THE SPELL, 1985 (cat. no. 27)
Pine, cedar, and steel, 56 x 84 x 65 in.
Collection of the artist

TWO INTO ONE, 1985 (cat. no. 28)
Painted pine, 74 x 63 in.
Lent in the memory of Beverly R. Rollnick, New York

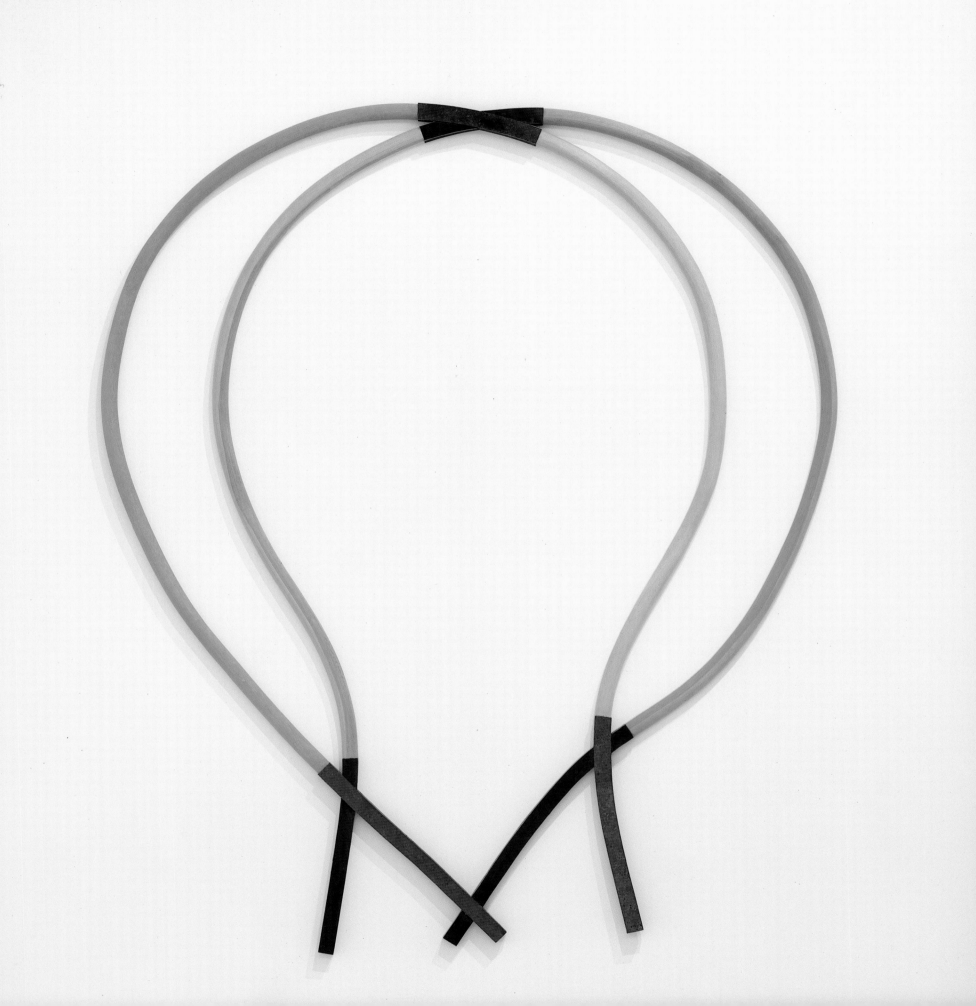

EMPIRE'S LURCH, 1987 (cat. no. 29)
Painted ponderosa pine, 75 × 48 × 25¼ in.
Private Collection, New York

NOBLESSE O., 1987 (cat. no. 30)
Red cedar and aluminum paint, 97 x 58 x 46 in.
Dallas Museum of Art, Central Acquisitions Fund and a gift of The 500, Inc.

SHARP AND FLAT, 1987 (cat. no. 31)
Pine, 64½ × 80 × 30 in.
Mr. and Mrs. Harry W. Anderson, Atherton, California

TIMBER'S TURN, 1987 (cat. no. 32)
Honduras mahogany, red cedar, and
Douglas fir, 87 × 61 × 48 in.
Hirshhorn Museum and Sculpture
Garden, Washington, D.C.,
Smithsonian Institution,
Museum Purchase, 1987

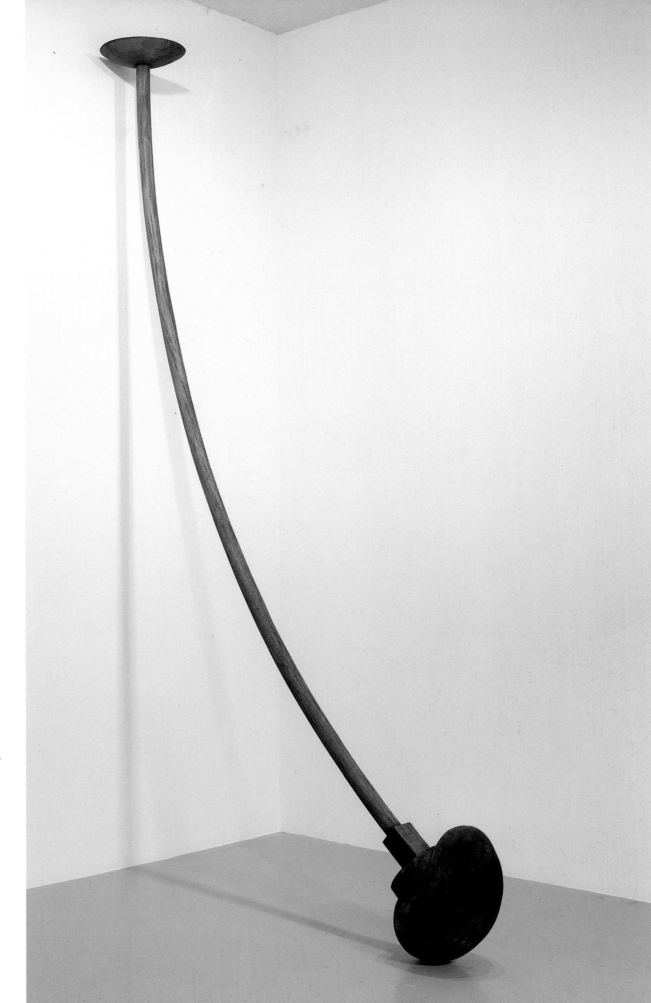

TO TRANSCEND, 1987 (cat. no. 33)
Stained Honduras mahogany and poplar,
9 ft. 7½ in. × 90 in. × 13 ft.
Walker Art Center, Minneapolis,
Walker Special Purchase Fund, 1988

UNTITLED, 1987 (cat. no. 34)
Tar, steel mesh, pine, and Douglas fir, 68 x 78 x 35 in.
Mrs. Vera List, New York

MAROON, 1987–88 (cat. no. 35)
Steel mesh, tar, pine, and yellow poplar, 76 in. × 10 ft. × 78 in.
Milwaukee Art Museum, Gift of Contemporary Art Society

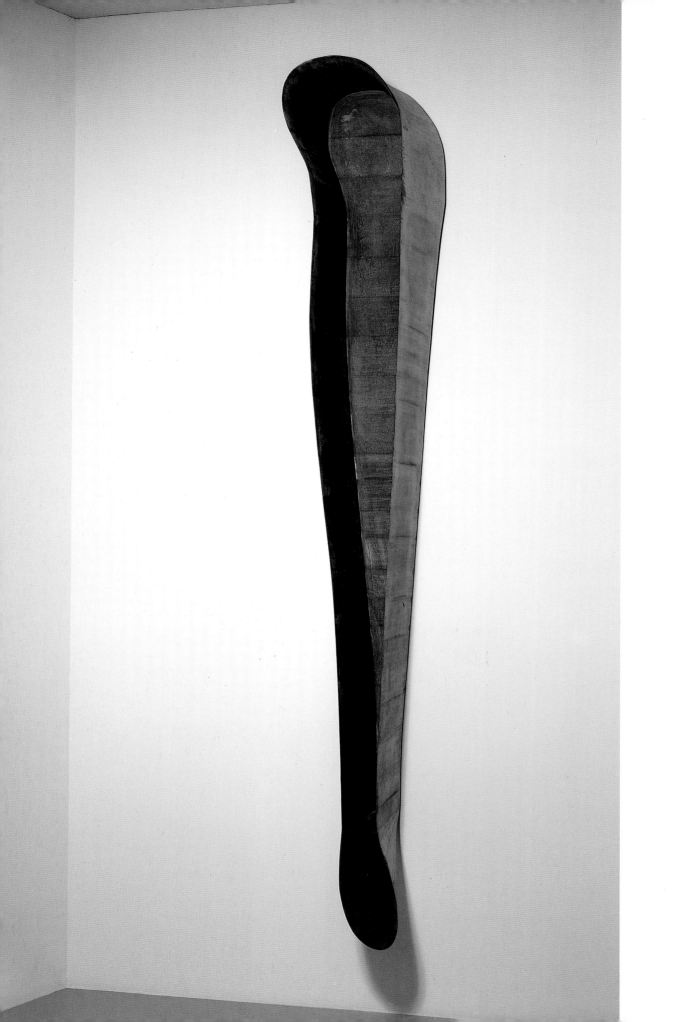

THE CUT, 1988 (cat. no. 36)
Painted red cedar and pine,
11 ft. 10 in. × 21 in. × 17 in.
The Nerman Collection, Courtesy of
The Nelson-Atkins Museum of Art,
Kansas City, Missouri

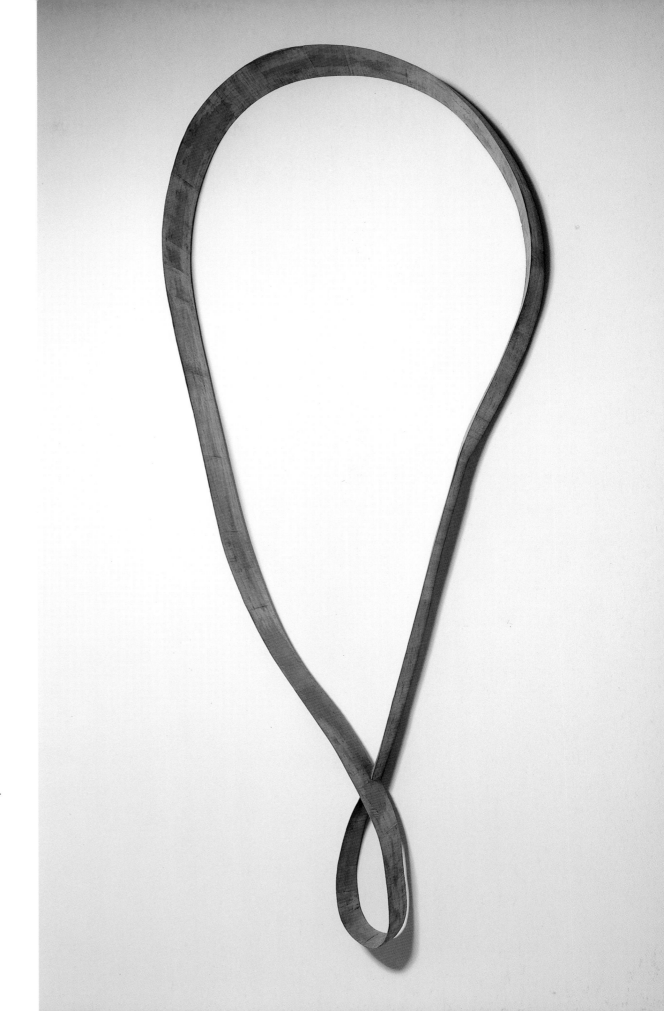

PRIDE'S CROSS, 1988 (cat. no. 37)
Red cedar and poplar, 9 ft. 9 in. × 48 in. × 11¼ in.
Private Collection, Baltimore

LEVER #1, 1988–89 (cat. no. 38)
Red cedar, 14 ft. 1 in. × 11 ft. 2 in. × 18 in.
The Art Institute of Chicago, A. James Speyer Memorial; with additional
funds provided by UNR Industries in honor of James W. Alsdorf, Barbara
and Solomon Byron Smith funds, 1989.385

LEVER #2, 1988–89 (cat. no. 39) (see pp. 122–23)
Rattan, ponderosa pine, ash, and cypress, 71 in. × 24 ft. 5 in. × 55 in.
The Baltimore Museum of Art, The Caplan Family Contemporary Art Fund,
and the Collector's Circle Fund

THICKET, 1990 (cat. no. 40)
Basswood and cypress, 67 × 62 × 17 in.
Seattle Art Museum, Gift of Agnes Gund, 90.32

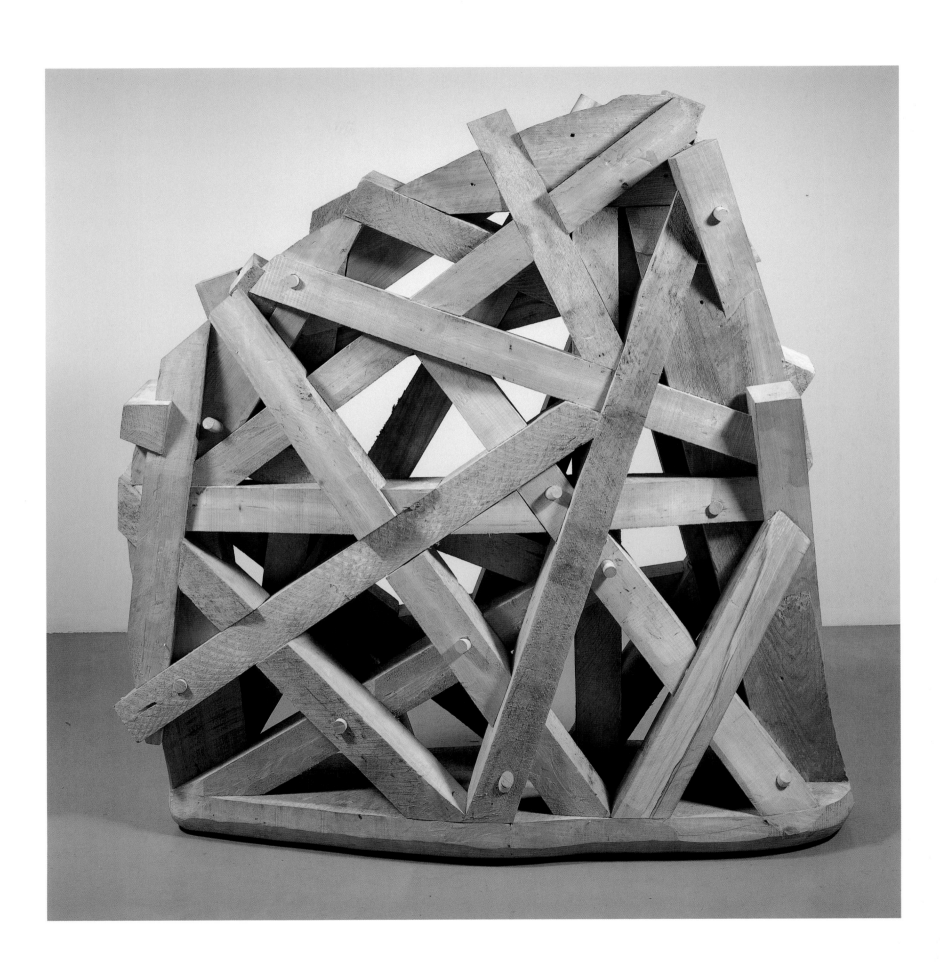

MARTIN PURYEAR: THE HAND'S PROPORTION

By Robert Storr

Martin Puryear, *She*, 1979
Red cedar and Douglas fir
8 ft. 10 in. high
California Afro-American Museum
Foundation, Gift of Linda and
Harry Macklowe

Art in the eighties generally assumed a decentered "subject." For most of the decade painters, photographers, and conceptualists of a "deconstructive" bent have gleaned, artfully misplaced, and endlessly recycled images of both high and low order. Their aim was to expose the plural and fragmented selfhood that is said to be the truth of our modern or postmodern condition. Haphazardly assembled from scraps of personal and public history, and constantly under the seductive assault of the media, "identity" glimmers and fades in the static glow of short-term memory. Sometimes intoxicated, sometimes horrified, but most often numbed by the sheer variety and evanescence of their experience, the "heroes" of this time are shells of the heroes of former times. They are souls fleetingly stirred and permanently disoriented by the free-floating energies of the moment.

Not so the "subject" of Martin Puryear's work. Responding to the same distractions and flux as his more skeptical and less stubborn contemporaries, Puryear envisions for his phantom surrogates a potential and all-embracing wholeness. The artist addresses this search for focused existence in the most pragmatic way, by constructing dwellings or markers, in or near which his imagined protagonist might finally, though perhaps only briefly, come to rest and recognition. From his suspended wooden circles and his meticulously fashioned sanctuaries to his compact monoliths, Puryear's sculpture always seeks and ultimately finds its center. And if, as is frequently the case, that core is empty, rather than symbolizing the void, such vacancy is an expectant one designating a site and a space awaiting its natural inhabitant.

Puryear's protagonist is a quiet one, and, although it may yearn for peace and perhaps transcendence, never, in the manner of the expressionist self, does it proclaim aloud its erstwhile struggles. Inasmuch as it can be taken to be the artist himself, Puryear's "subject" is a self-effacing one, happy to be lost in the task of preparing its physical and spiritual redoubt. Of major sculptors active today, Puryear is, in fact, exceptional in the extremes to which he goes to remove personal narrative from the aura of his pieces. Nevertheless, he succeeds in charging them with an intense and palpable necessity born of his absolute authority over and assiduous involvement in their execution. This desire for anonymity is akin to that of the traditional craftsman whose private identity is subsumed in the realized identity of his creations rather than being consumed in a pyrotechnic drama of the artistic ego. As embodied in Puryear's sculpture, however, this workmanlike reticence allied to an utter stylistic clarity is as puzzling and as evocative as a Zen *koan*.

Subtle and imperative, the existential paradoxes of Zen are regularly couched in humorous terms. So too, Puryear's sculptures are frequently witty and, like any well-conceived riddle, they are always elegant in their simplicity. On occasion, whimsical turns of phrase, rhymes, and puns show up in his titles as well. *Sharp and Flat*, 1987 (cat. no. 31), thus invokes a musical metaphor, yet its honed edges and faceted surfaces are palpably those named. In a similar vein, *Where the Heart Is (Sleeping Mews)*, which includes bird effigies, plays upon the term "mews" — that is, cages for moulting hawks — and the evocativeness of its homonym, "muse." More often, Puryear's forms evidence a calm determination to contradict expectations. For example, despite its dense monumental presence, the dark and imposing piece *Self*, 1978 (cat. no. 7), is, in reality, quite hollow. We are dealing with an art of exquisite nuance and confident reserve, an art that is exceedingly refined but untainted by the slightest pretense or the least self-satisfaction.

Puryear's is a cosmopolitan art as well, befitting its much traveled but always well-grounded creator. Intellectual or imaginative pursuits rather than nomadic restlessness or alienated self-exile explain his movements. A volunteer teacher in Africa, a student in Scandinavia, a Guggenheim Fellow in Japan, and a resident at various times of Washington, Chicago, New Haven, New York City, and now semirural upstate New York, Puryear has moved about freely, but he has settled comfortably in each of the several places he has lived. These periodic relocations have been prompted by an omnivorous curiosity that has direct and obvious bearing on his art. To an extent rare among the contemporary scene's globe-trotting artists, moreover, Puryear has made himself at home in both the "First" and "Third" worlds, in the process becoming a keen witness to the constant cross-fertilization among their many, very different, and continuously evolving societies.

It comes as no surprise, then, that Puryear has directed his attention to the story of Jim Beckwourth, the child of an African-American woman and a white man, who lived as a frontiersman and eventually became a chief of the Crow Indians. The earth and board *tumulus* that the artist has dedicated to him (see cat. no. 13) is in effect a monument to the history of cultural interminglings that nationalist ideologies of all kinds hasten to obscure. Like Beckwourth, the agents of the integrated history that Puryear honors are people who have shown that the fusion of separate traditions and ethnic groups may be forced upon them by circumstance but can be fully and positively realized by acknowledged affinity and active empathy. Moreover, such fusions need not automatically reflect — and may instead counter, undo, or obviate — the conventions of the dominant culture. Now as during previous periods of crisis, chauvinist pressures are again being exerted on every side, by long-marginalized and often angrily alienated communities, but most especially by "mainstream" ideologues hysterically fearful that they lose their bearings — and be lost sight of — in the open sea of a truly multicultural republic. In such a setting, Puryear's hard-won belief in, even optimism about, the possibility of cultural synthesis is welcome indeed. Through the Beckwourth pieces as through his work generally, the artist pointedly alerts us to the fact that the creation and assumption of an individual identity results less from the overwhelming influence of one aspect of our background or consciousness over all others than from an admission that "difference" exists not merely between us but within each of us. In place of a metaphysical universal, therefore, the whole we seek is a collaboration of the disparate parts and a counterpoint of many inner voices.

It follows that the "subject" of Puryear's work is polyglot, as is the man who made it. The artist prefers to speak with his hands, however, although they too are "polyglot." In Sierra Leone from 1964 to 1966 where he taught biology, English, and French for the Peace Corps, he learned the basics of carpentry from local workmen in a fair and symbiotic exchange of expertise. He followed up on this experience by studying printmaking at the Royal Academy in Sweden between 1966 and 1968, as well as independently pursuing furniture-making at the source of "Scandinavian contemporary" design. Having concentrated on painting as an undergraduate at Catholic University in Washington, D.C., prior to these years abroad, Puryear thus secured a uniquely varied and in-depth training in the simple techniques of building and the complex art of joinery, before devoting himself entirely to advanced studies in sculpture at Yale University.

By then, Puryear's choice of wood as a primary material was firm. For him the basic attraction lay in its variety of hue, density, and tensile strength, as well as in its original and abiding vitality, one which forever remains subject to movement and change in response to different environments and methods of handling. In keeping with these criteria, Puryear has since added to the already rich inventory of woods a number of other staples of related pliability, diverse coloration, and texture, such as rope, deerskins, and rawhide strips. The last two, for instance, he used in the large-scale installation piece *Equation for Jim Beckwourth* (1980), from which several components survive (see cat. nos. 1, 8, 13). Lately, in pieces from the "Stereotypes and Decoys" series, such as *Untitled*, 1987, and *Maroon*, 1987–88 (cat. nos. 34, 35), he has turned to tar and mesh, which, although refined, synthesized, or factory-produced materials, possess formal and plastic properties similar to the natural stuffs with which he began. In most cases, the deciding factor appears to have been that the resources used be strong but easily workable, lightweight but capable of being transformed, by bending, binding, stretching, or lamination, into self-supporting structures.

After several generations of steel sculpture in which massiveness, whether earthbound or gravity defying, was an essential aesthetic as well as engineering quality of the object, this recourse to organic substances and open-ribbed or husklike construction was unexpected. Modernism, many had come to believe in the 1960s and 1970s, was synonymous with the use of industrial technology and industrial finishes; paying requisite heed to contemporary reality meant employing if not testing the limits of the methods of fabrication made possible by the machine age. Augmented by the pressures of supply and demand and the allure of "multiples," art went into production. The most recent manifestation of this shift from studio to factory output now plays itself out in strategies of "commodity art," in which even the idea of creating a unique prototype has been all but abandoned. Placing Minimalist enumeration and facture at the service of Pop imagery, sculptors have imitated and lampooned the strategies of marketing.

Puryear, whose career began in the aftermath of Minimalism and whose art is now reaching its full fruition in the age of appropriation, is a maker not a manufacturer of sculptures. As such, he has been something of an anomaly. The generation and tendency to which he nevertheless belongs has had a pervasive, albeit diffuse, impact on the language and content of sculpture over the last twenty years. Because of the stylistic diversity of its exemplars, however, that influence has often been overshadowed by the more codified practice of the Minimalist and Neo-Dada schools that chronologically bracket it. Useful comparison can be made between Puryear's oeuvre and that of a number of his near or exact contemporaries. Included are Nancy Graves's conjugations of camel forms and ritual objects, Jackie Winsor's bound and laminated modules, Joel Shapiro's dense dwellings, blocked figures, and cantilevered abstractions, as well as the framed, planked, and eccentrically scaled enclosures of Alice Aycock, Jackie Ferrara, Mary Miss, and Siah Armajani.

Common to all, but perhaps most pronounced in the work of Puryear, Graves, and Aycock, has been an avidity for "information." Along with Conceptualists and Minimalists, they have shared a desire to escape the strictures of their own or conventional "taste" by exploring "nonartistic" sources while adhering in the studio to more or less systemic procedures. These artists deal primarily in images and empirically discovered methods rather than strictly formal propositions or logical or linguistic equations. "Book learning," however, is key to the wide range of concerns and disciplines to which their work refers. Puryear and his peers have especially favored the fields of ethnography and natural history — using their research skills to recover, reimagine, and breathe new life into paradigms usually confined to the realm of scientific or social scientific enquiry. University-educated to a degree generally unprecedented in the history of Modernism, they have produced work that echoes with the discourse of the library as much as it does that of the art museum. It is a subtle Borgesian discourse of magical correspondences remarked upon with a paradoxical yet decided matter-of-factness.

Routinely drawing our attention to the means used to realize his work, Puryear, like the others, has thus been content to let his conceptual process show as well, making no attempt to disguise his sources of inspiration. Quite the opposite, he has readily acknowledged the intriguingly various archetypes to which his work alludes, from vernacular architecture in the yurt *Where the Heart Is (Sleeping Mews)* and the giant wheel and capstan structure *Desire*, 1981 (see p. 12), to the African-inspired bronze chair that anchors his largest outdoor environment, *Bodark Arc*, 1982. If, in the spirit of the times, the work of this least ironic of sculptors harbors a latent Duchampian component, it is, as Jonathan Crary has pointed out, the way in which Puryear has transmogrified the shapes or images he has selected into a kind of anthropological "assisted ready-made."[1]

What is crucial, finally, is the particular manner and exact degree to which each has been "assisted." In some, the alteration consists of grafting appropriated elements unto others normally "foreign" to them, thereby creating a poetic composite greater and more mysterious than the sum of its parts. Such complex interweaving or overlaying of disparate elements is especially typical of his sometimes elaborate installations. More recently, Puryear has tended to distill his "found" forms until they occupy an indeterminate but powerfully evocative position between vestigial representation and pure abstraction. Made shortly before he devoted his energy to fashioning rings and hoops such as *Big and Little Same*, *Dream of Pairing*, *Untitled*, and *Endgame* (cat. nos. 14–16, 24), the two-pronged *Stripling* of 1976 (cat. no. 5) engages, as these subsequent pieces do, in the dialectic between enclosure and openness. Yet for all the abstractness of its form, the work retains a vaguely practical aspect, as if it were a hewn and fitted tool from an earlier era. Like several roughly contemporary pieces, in fact, *Stripling* suggests a caliper for measuring dimensions such as a classical modeler or marble sculptor might use, or a compass capable of charting the circles Puryear not long thereafter began to make.

The back-and-forth exchange between representation and abstraction appears to have moved in the opposite direction in several pieces completed during the last few years. Instead of departing from preexisting shapes or images, Puryear evidently approached them from the point of view of a more purely nonobjective interest in the disposition of lines and volumes. Relating curved or jutting extensions to finely contoured volumetric forms in *Empire's Lurch*, *Sharp and Flat*, *Timber's Turn*, *Untitled*, all of 1987 (cat. nos. 29, 31, 32, 34), and *Lever #1*, 1988–89 (cat. no. 38), the artist seems to have first arrived at a compositional balance only to recognize in that configuration the attenuated and eccentrically essentialized image of a duck hunter's decoy. In shape, surface, or manner of construction, other works recall other natural or manmade referents. *Self*, *Cask Cascade* (cat. no. 23), *Old Mole* (cat. no. 25), and the finial of *Seer*, 1984, all suggest claws, teeth, or beaks. *Greed's Trophy* and *Keeper*, both of 1984 (cat. nos. 19, 20), are reminiscent of certain types of fishing net or jai alai rackets. *Believer*, 1977–82 (cat. no. 6), and *Maroon*, 1987–88, resemble gourds.

As richly allusive as these abstractions are, definitive knowledge of their probable sources or nearest analogue is unnecessary for, perhaps even antithetical to, an appreciation of their aesthetic resolution. The symbolic or mimetic indeterminacy they enjoy is counterpoised, however, to the rigorous specificity of their facture. This explicit preoccupation with details of facture and finish is a means not an end, a form of address not just a private obsession. For Puryear, a work cannot be fully intelligible unless it appeals to and enters our consciousness via the senses. A firm believer in the primacy of visual and tactile modes of communicating not just aesthetic pleasure but the wealth of information and associations inscribed in the materials he employs and the shapes he delineates, Puryear "assists" his "ready-made" images and distinguishes and elaborates upon his basic abstract forms by a determined accentuation of their physical nuances and presence.

The care he lavishes upon piecing together and embellishing his work harkens back to notions of artisanal integrity that stir an uneasiness in those for whom the unmarked boundary between art and craft represents persistently problematic reality. Puryear shares that uneasiness neither in principle nor in practice. Quite the opposite, he manifestly enjoys the freedoms afforded him by the lack of any certainty about where one domain ends and the other begins. He has in fact dedicated his time to filling in and so enlarging the no man's land which joins them with markers that further confound attempts to fix an exact frontier. If any criterion adequately resolves the distinction between "fine" and "applied" art, it is probably one based upon a division of "useless" from "useful" objects, to which former category Puryear's sculpture would appear to belong. Except, of course, that things addressed to or accommodating of the "spirit" are only considered "useless" in societies such as ours which take a narrowly materialist account of experience and need.

A similar set of definitional dilemmas arises when we look toward those societies where such a separation between "inspirited" and "functional" form is not made, societies that the modern world commonly flatters itself by thinking of as "primitive." Puryear is acutely and instructively aware of these issues. Having freely drawn upon precedents from traditional as well as industrialized cultures, and having clearly intended that his pieces orient viewers both inwardly and outwardly in order that they might redefine their sense of being in the world, Puryear has never patronized the "originators" of the models he has adopted and recast, nor has he sought to cloak his sculpture in an archaic mantle. To the contrary, he has spurned the role of art world shaman. Indeed, the diffidence of his persona and the pragmatism he has applied to his task underscore Puryear's regard for the secretive "soul" of his creations and his deference toward that which occupies the creations of others.

Puryear's experience in Sierra Leone is especially telling in this regard. Welcomed into the community he found there, Puryear nonetheless understood implicitly that although an African-American, he, as much as anyone of European extraction, was an outsider to the customs of the people among whom he lived. Loathe to intrude upon their tribal observances, and apparently disinclined to subscribe to ideological notions of "Negritude," Puryear forswore any attempt to study firsthand the carving of effigies or artifacts whose rendering entailed a knowledge of ritual secrets to which he was not and would never be party. Instead he dedicated himself to learning the "trade secrets" of the local builders, which raised no such problems of cultural expropriation or improper pastiche. An appreciation of the mastery he recognized in their work and hoped to emulate not only helps to explain the complex mechanisms of assimilation in Puryear's own sculpture, but calls for reexamination of the relation of "Third World" to "First World" societies, just as it draws attention to commonplace misconceptions about the contribution of "primitivism" to "modernism."

Even recourse to such dichotomous categories is presently the subject of intense, often bitter, contention. For generations, however, painters and sculptors from the urban, industrial world have projected their Edenic fantasies onto non-Western cultures without owning up to or even questioning the obvious implications of the "poetic" license taken. Persistent precisely because of the denials it simultaneously requires and permits, the myth of the "primitive" forbids intimate acquaintance with the people to whom the rubric is applied and still more any recognition of their own self-consciousness. In lieu of a vital and changing reality, it presupposes a static *alter*reality poised between primordial *un*development and perpetual *under*development. Mesmerized by such notions, European and American artists have attempted to renew overcultivated aesthetic habits by injecting them with raw energy extracted from "primitive" models, while at the same time priding themselves on raising low forms to high, non-art to the status of art.[2]

Staple concepts of the "primitive" or the exotic like these have been the furthest thing from Puryear's mind. What he has sought and found in his various investigations into artisanal traditions has not been rhetorical "crudeness" but the opposite. His exchange with the builders of Sierra Leone, like that engaged in with the cabinetmakers of Sweden, was a dialogue of sophisticates. The ultimate point has never been to mimic rustic technologies or gloss atavistic symbols so as to invoke or recreate an anachronistic world. The point has instead been to recover the creative possibilities offered by highly refined crafts that have been marginalized by industrial society, or simply lost to it.

That marginalization has usually been accompanied by condescension, and even hostility. Of late, in fact, the concept of "mastery" has fallen into almost total disrepute, becoming little more than an epithet for the ostentatious display of facility, and/or a code-word for "patriarchal" privilege. Puryear's demonstrated mastery challenges this by now routine dismissal of the idea in physical and idiomatic terms. A command of form and materials such as his cannot be paraphrased away into a neat theoretical package and thereby disposed of. Dignifying once again the work of hands, Puryear's sculpture is a vivid reminder that such dignity must be earned and such skills patiently acquired. To speak of mastery does not suppose an innate capacity nor assert a suspect claim to "genius." It simply names the culmination of a prolonged and utterly practical education, marked in stages by the passage of an individual from apprenticeship to the status of journeyman and from there to the complete, "masterful" grasp of his or her discipline. Puryear's mastery was prepared in just this manner, and the freedom it has given him is plain to see. Oddly in this regard, Puryear's closest peer among living sculptors is Richard Artschwager, the Josef Hoffmann of formica, although the late H. C. Westermann, fastidious funk-joiner of wood and arch nonjoiner of art movements, comes closer still.

All who, like Puryear, undertake to establish a fresh congruence between traditional facture and modern forms owe a debt to Brancusi, in whose work the opposition of "primitive" and "sophisticate" was perhaps first and most forcefully contested. After initially achieving distinction as an urbane Rodinesque modeler, Brancusi utterly transformed modern sculpture by using the techniques of the woodworker and stonemason to create art of the ultimate chic and, literally, the utmost polish. The peasantlike perseverance Brancusi showed in working with the grain of his materials but against that of prevailing studio conventions calls into question the much discussed "fetishization" of the contemporary art object, and suggests that another than purely commercial economy is at issue.

It is the same economy that determines the formal quality and imminent character of Puryear's work as well. Neither the maker of fetishes nor the producer of commodities, Puryear has set aside the cult of absent demiurges or transcendent aestheticism in order to devote his complete attention to poetic presence. With the same determination he has turned his back on the temptations of production and consumption to devote his full energies to "making." The economics of Puryear's art are, therefore, those of time. Not time-as-money, but the time it takes to gain sure and intimate knowledge of a task directly at hand, and the prolonged scrutiny required to articulate the specifics demanded by a clear vision of one's aim. Against this standard, judging Puryear's achievement, and to the same extent that of any artist, might best be thought of in terms of gauging with one's own mind and eye the degree to which the objects we encounter repay in kind and in full the investment in concentration we have made in them. At present, the rapid turnover in styles and rapid turnovers in gallery inventories tend to discourage contemplation. By default, only art that services impulse looking, and hence unequivocally accepts and exploits the terms of its own explicit superficiality and redundance, seems "realistic." Until, that is, one comes upon a genuine exception. Puryear's preternaturally unhurried work constitutes just such an exception, quietly restoring the belief that even at this frenetic moment, time, slowed to the pace of an alert and self-possessed imagination, may yet be on our side.

NOTES

I would like to thank Kellie Jones of the Jamaica Arts Center, Jamaica, New York, for permission to rework and republish this text, which she originally commissioned for the 1989 catalogue accompanying the survey of Puryear's work for the "20ª Bienal Internacional de São Paulo." I am also grateful to Michael Brenson, art critic of *The New York Times*, for much of the biographical information used in this essay, as well as for his critical appraisal of a body of work he has championed with singular conviction and eloquence.

1. Jonathan Crary, "Martin Puryear's Sculpture," *Artforum* 18,2 (October 1979), pp. 28–31.

2. For the best introduction to and most thoughtful examination of recent debate over the uses and especially the abuses of the term "primitive," see James Clifford, *The Predicament of Culture: Twentieth Century Ethnography, Literature and Art* (Cambridge, Massachusetts, and London: Harvard University Press, 1988).

DOCUMENTATION

CATALOGUE OF THE EXHIBITION

Because Martin Puryear has on occasion altered his sculptures, even after exhibition, they may span a period of several years before their final forms are resolved.

1. RAWHIDE CONE, 1974 (second version, 1980; original destroyed in 1977)
    Rawhide
    51 × 63 × 32 in.
    Collection of the artist

2. SOME TALES, 1975–77
    Ash and yellow pine
    30 ft. long (approximately)
    Panza di Biumo Collection, Milan

3. BASK, 1976
    Staved dyed pine
    12 in. × 12 ft. 2¾ in. × 24 in.
    Solomon R. Guggenheim Museum, New York, Exxon Corporation Purchase Award

4. CIRCUMBENT, 1976
    Ash
    64 in. × 9 ft. 11¾ in. × 21 in.
    Collection of the artist

5. STRIPLING, 1976
    Ash
    85 × 10 in.
    Truland Systems Corporation, Arlington, Virginia

6. BELIEVER, 1977–82
    Poplar and pine
    23¼ × 23⅜ × 17⅜ in.
    Collection of the artist

7. SELF, 1978
    Painted cedar and mahogany
    69 × 48 × 25 in.
    Joslyn Art Museum, Omaha, Nebraska, Purchase in memory of Elinor Ashton

8. SOME LINES FOR JIM BECKWOURTH, 1978
    Twisted rawhide
    23 ft. long (approximately)
    Collection of the artist
    (Chicago, Los Angeles, and Philadelphia only)

9. UNTITLED, 1978
    African blackwood and vine
    15⅞ in. long
    Truland Systems Corporation, Arlington, Virginia

10. UNTITLED, 1978
    Hickory and Alaskan yellow cedar
    60 × 78 × 1 in.
    Nancy and Douglas Drysdale, Washington, D.C.

11. PRIMAVERA, 1979
    Painted pine and maple
    64¾ × 64 × 2 in.
    Nancy A. Drysdale, Washington, D.C.
    (Chicago, Los Angeles, and Philadelphia only)

12. BOWER, 1980
    Pine and Sitka spruce
    64 × 94¾ × 26⅝ in.
    The Oliver-Hoffmann Collection, Chicago

13. FOR BECKWOURTH, 1980
    Earth, pitch pine, and oak
    40 × 34 × 34 in.
    Collection of the artist

14. BIG AND LITTLE SAME, 1981
    Ponderosa pine, painted pine, and unpainted pear wood
    61 × 62 × 2¾ in.
    Councilman Joel Wachs, Los Angeles

15. DREAM OF PAIRING, 1981
    Painted pine
    51½ × 54½ × 2 in.
    Alice Kleberg Reynolds, Artemis Investments, San Antonio, Texas

16. UNTITLED, 1981–82
    Painted ponderosa pine
    58 in. diameter × 9⅜ in.
    Murray Bring, New York

17. SANCTUARY, 1982
    Pine, maple, and cherry
    10 ft. 6 in. × 24 in. × 18 in.
    The Art Institute of Chicago, Mr. and Mrs. Frank G. Logan Prize Fund, 1982.1473

18. UNTITLED, 1982
    Maple sapling, pear wood, and yellow cedar
    59 × 66 × 5 in.
    Judith and Edward Neisser, Chicago

19. GREED'S TROPHY, 1984
    Hickory, ebony, rattan, steel, and wire
    12 ft. 9 in. × 20 in. × 55 in.
    The Museum of Modern Art, New York, David Rockefeller Fund and Purchase

20. KEEPER, 1984
    Pine and steel wire
    8 ft. 4 in. × 34 in. × 38 in.
    Alan and Wendy Hart, Topanga, California

21. LURK, 1984
Painted pine
21¾ × 61¼ × 7¼ in.
Collection of Margo Leavin, Los Angeles

22. NIGHT AND DAY, 1984
Painted pine and wire
75 in. × 10 ft. × 6 in.
The Patsy N. and Raymond D. Nasher Collection, Dallas

23. CASK CASCADE, 1985
Painted red cedar
61¾ × 59½ × 30¼ in.
John and Mary Pappajohn, Des Moines, Iowa

24. ENDGAME, 1985
Painted pine
65 × 66 × 5 in.
REFCO Group, Ltd., Chicago

25. OLD MOLE, 1985
Red cedar
61 × 61 × 32 in.
Philadelphia Museum of Art: Purchased: The Samuel S. White, 3rd,
and Vera White Collection (by exchange) and Gift of Mr. and Mrs.
C. G. Chaplin (by exchange) and funds contributed by Marion
Stroud Swingle, and funds contributed by friends and family in
memory of Mrs. H. Gates Lloyd

26. SANCTUM, 1985
Pine, wire mesh, and tar
76 in. × 9 ft. 1 in. × 87 in.
Whitney Museum of American Art, New York, Purchase, with
funds from the Painting and Sculpture Committee, 85.72

27. THE SPELL, 1985
Pine, cedar, and steel
56 × 84 × 65 in.
Collection of the artist
(Chicago, Los Angeles, and Philadelphia only)

28. TWO INTO ONE, 1985
Painted pine
74 × 63 in.
Lent in the memory of Beverly R. Rollnick, New York

29. EMPIRE'S LURCH, 1987
Painted ponderosa pine
75 × 48 × 25¼ in.
Private Collection, New York

30. NOBLESSE O., 1987
Red cedar and aluminum paint
97 × 58 × 46 in.
Dallas Museum of Art, Central Acquisitions Fund and a gift of
The 500, Inc.

31. SHARP AND FLAT, 1987
Pine
64½ × 80 × 30 in.
Mr. and Mrs. Harry W. Anderson, Atherton, California
(Chicago, Washington, D.C., and Los Angeles only)

32. TIMBER'S TURN, 1987
Honduras mahogany, red cedar, and Douglas fir
87 × 61 × 48 in.
Hirshhorn Museum and Sculpture Garden, Washington, D.C.,
Smithsonian Institution, Museum Purchase, 1987

33. TO TRANSCEND, 1987
Stained Honduras mahogany and poplar
9 ft. 7½ in. × 90 in. × 13 ft.
Walker Art Center, Minneapolis, Walker Special Purchase
Fund, 1988
(Chicago, Los Angeles, and Philadelphia only)

34. UNTITLED, 1987
Tar, steel mesh, pine, and Douglas fir
68 × 78 × 35 in.
Mrs. Vera List, New York

35. MAROON, 1987–88
Steel mesh, tar, pine, and yellow poplar
76 in. × 10 ft. × 78 in.
Milwaukee Art Museum, Gift of Contemporary Art Society

36. THE CUT, 1988
Painted red cedar and pine
11 ft. 10 in. × 21 in. × 17 in.
The Nerman Collection, Courtesy of The Nelson-Atkins Museum
of Art, Kansas City, Missouri

37. PRIDE'S CROSS, 1988
Red cedar and poplar
9 ft. 9 in. × 48 in. × 11¼ in.
Private Collection, Baltimore

38. LEVER #1, 1988–89
Red cedar
14 ft. 1 in. × 11 ft. 2 in. × 18 in.
The Art Institute of Chicago, A. James Speyer Memorial; with
additional funds provided by UNR Industries in honor of James W.
Alsdorf, Barbara and Solomon Byron Smith funds, 1989.385

39. LEVER #2, 1988–89
Rattan, ponderosa pine, ash, and cypress
71 in. × 24 ft. 5 in. × 55 in.
The Baltimore Museum of Art, The Caplan Family Contemporary
Art Fund, and the Collector's Circle Fund

40. THICKET, 1990
Basswood and cypress
67 × 62 × 17 in.
Seattle Art Museum, Gift of Agnes Gund, 90.32

CHRONOLOGY

1941

Martin Puryear was born on May 23 in Washington, D.C. He is the oldest of seven children with four brothers and two sisters. His father, Reginald, is a retired postal employee and his mother, Martina, is a retired elementary teacher. When he was in elementary school, Puryear won a scholarship to a children's art school run by Cornelia Yuditsky. As a young man, he built guitars, furniture, and canoes.

1959–63

Puryear entered Catholic University of America in Washington, D.C., in the fall of 1959 as a biology major. He changed his major to art during his junior year and graduated in 1963 with a Bachelor of Arts degree. While at Catholic University he studied painting and the philosophy of art with Nell B. Sonneman and was exposed to the Color-Field paintings of Kenneth Noland who was also a faculty member. In 1962 he participated in a group exhibition at the Adams-Morgan Gallery in Washington, D.C. Puryear won an award for one of his entries in the Maryland Regional Exhibition held at The Baltimore Museum of Art in 1963. He also spent some time in New York where he visited The Museum of Modern Art, the Whitney Museum of American Art, and The Metropolitan Museum of Art.

1964–66

Following graduation from college, Puryear joined the Peace Corps and traveled to Sierra Leone in West Africa to teach art, biology, English, and French at a secondary school in the remote village of Segbwema. Here, Puryear observed craftspeople, including weavers, potters, cloth dyers, and carpenters. He worked with carpenters to learn techniques of wood craftsmanship such as joinery.

1966–68

Puryear was accepted at the Swedish Royal Academy of Art in Stockholm to study printmaking and received a Scandinavian-American Foundation Study Grant. He did graphic work during the day and studied sculpture independently in the evenings. Puryear also explored Scandinavian crafts and learned about the tools and techniques of furniture-making. He was introduced to fine woodworking in the studio of the furniture-maker James Krenov. He participated in both the 1967 and the 1968 Annual Exhibition of the Swedish Royal Academy of Art, as well as in the 1968 Stockholm Biennial. In 1968 Puryear had his first individual exhibition, at the Gröna Palletten Gallery. During this period he traveled extensively in Lapland and Scandinavia and visited Moscow. In the summer of 1968 he attended the Venice Biennale and upon his return to the United States worked briefly as a designer for SCAN, a Scandinavian furniture company.

1969–71

In the fall of 1969, Puryear received a grant for graduate study in sculpture at Yale University in New Haven, Connecticut. Puryear studied with Al Held and James Rosati, who were Yale faculty members, as well as with Robert Morris, Salvatore Scarpitta, Richard Serra, and Richard Van Buren, who were visiting artists. He also took a course with Robert

Martin Puryear in his studio, Chicago, 1987

Farris Thompson, a historian of African art. He visited Soho for the first time and familiarized himself with contemporary American art, particularly Minimalism. He graduated from Yale in 1971 with a Master of Fine Arts degree.

1971–73

Puryear joined the faculty of Fisk University, Nashville, Tennessee, as an Assistant Professor of Art. In 1972 his first individual exhibition in the United States was held at the Henri 2 Gallery in Washington, D.C. This exhibition also marked the first time his sculpture was shown in a gallery. In the fall of 1973, he established a studio in Brooklyn, New York.

1974–78

Puryear taught as an Assistant Professor of Art at the University of Maryland, College Park, through 1978. During this period Puryear received several grants, including two Creative and Performing Artists

Grants from the University of Maryland (1975, 1978); a Creative Artists Public Service Grant for sculpture from the New York Creative Artists Public Service Program (1976); a Change, Inc., Robert Rauschenberg Foundation Grant (1977); and a National Endowment for the Arts, Individual Artist Fellowship (1978). In 1977 The Corcoran Gallery of Art, Washington, D.C., presented a one-person exhibition of Puryear's sculpture. His work was also included in the "Young American Artists, 1978 Exxon National Exhibition," at The Solomon R. Guggenheim Museum, New York. Protetch-McIntosh Gallery of Washington, D.C., also showed his work in 1978.

In 1977 *Box and Pole*, his first major outdoor sculpture commission, was completed for Artpark in Lewiston, New York. Also, in February of 1977 a fire in his Brooklyn studio destroyed or damaged most of his sculpture. He was awarded a studio for one year at the Institute for Art and Urban Resources, P.S. 1, Long Island City, New York. In the fall of 1978, Puryear moved to Chicago where he taught at the University of Illinois at Chicago.

1979–81

During the fall of 1979, Puryear was in residence at Yaddo, the artists' community in Saratoga Springs, New York. Just after this sojourn, his first ring sculptures were exhibited at Protetch-McIntosh Gallery in Washington, D.C. His work was also included in both the 1979 and 1981 Biennial Exhibitions at the Whitney Museum of American Art, New York. In 1980 Puryear installed *Equation for Jim Beckwourth* for an individual exhibition at the Museum of Contemporary Art, Chicago. Other individual exhibitions of Puryear's work in 1980 were held at the Young Hoffman Gallery, Chicago, and at the Joslyn Art Museum, Omaha. Puryear's *Where the Heart Is (Sleeping Mews)* was installed in 1981 at the and/or gallery in Seattle.

Puryear received a National Endowment for the Arts Planning Grant for Art in Public Places, and proposed several significant public art projects during this period. In 1979 he installed *Equivalents* at the Wave Hill Environmental Center and Sculpture Gardens in Bronx, New York. *Knoll for NOAA* was another major outdoor project: Puryear was one of five artists selected to work on a program of public art for the new facility of the National Oceanic and Atmospheric Administration in Seattle. Other public projects were the *Proposal for Duncan Plaza*, New Orleans, and *Pavilion-in-the-Trees* for Cliveden Park, Philadelphia.

1982–84

Two additional public sculpture projects were executed in 1982. The first was *Bodark Arc*, commissioned for the Nathan Manilow Sculpture Park at Governors State University, University Park, Illinois. Puryear also executed a commission for Gettysburg College, Gettysburg, Pennsylvania; this piece, titled *Sentinel*, is a massive form made of fieldstone. In that same year he exhibited in the "74th American Exhibition," at The Art Institute of Chicago.

Puryear was commissioned to make a poster for the Los Angeles 1984 Olympic Games. He also received a Louis Comfort Tiffany Grant, and a John S. Guggenheim Memorial Foundation Grant. The Guggenheim Foundation Grant enabled him to travel to Japan where he studied Japanese domestic architecture and gardens.

In 1984 a ten-year survey exhibition of Puryear's sculpture was organized by and presented at the University Gallery of the University of Massachusetts at Amherst. The exhibition traveled to The Berkshire Museum, Pittsfield, Massachusetts; the Museum of the National Center of Afro-American Artists, Boston; the New Museum of Contemporary Art, New York; and the La Jolla Museum of Contemporary Art, La Jolla, California. Also in 1984 Puryear's work was included in "An International Survey of Recent Painting and Sculpture" and "Primitivism in 20th Century Art: Affinity of the Tribal and the Modern," both at The Museum of Modern Art, New York.

1985–87

Puryear exhibited works in the 1985 "Transformations in Sculpture: Four Decades in American and European Art," at The Solomon R. Guggenheim Museum, New York. During the same year he had his first individual exhibition at the Margo Leavin Gallery, Los Angeles. In 1987 Puryear had his first individual gallery exhibition in New York at the David McKee Gallery. He also had an individual exhibition, titled "Martin Puryear: Public and Personal," at the Chicago Public Library Cultural Center.

Puryear continued to execute public sculpture and installed *River Road Ring* at the River Road Station of the Chicago Transit Authority as part of the City of Chicago Percent for Art Program. Another interior project, titled *Ark*, was installed at York College, The City University of New York, Jamaica, in 1986. Outdoor projects included *No Small Plans*, for the Penn Park Station, Port Authority of Allegheny County, Pittsburgh; *Stone Bow*, at Tufts University, Medford, Massachusetts; and *Ampersand* at the Minneapolis Sculpture Garden, Walker Art Center, Minneapolis. Puryear also worked with the architect Leo A. Daly to design the fountain, benches, pavilion, and a system of arbors and trellises at the Chevy Chase Garden Plaza, Chevy Chase, Maryland, a project that was completed in 1990.

In 1986 Puryear and Jeanne Gordon were married. Gordon is a classical pianist and an artist. Also in 1986 Puryear was in residence at the American Academy in Rome as a visiting artist.

1988–90

Puryear received the Francis J. Greenburger Foundation Award in 1988. He was selected as the sole United States representative for the 1989 São Paulo Bienal and was awarded the grand prize. Also in 1989 Puryear was awarded a John D. and Catherine T. MacArthur Foundation Fellowship, and was among the winners of the 33rd Annual Creative Arts Awards for Sculpture, Brandeis University, Waltham, Massachusetts. His work was included in the 1989 Whitney Biennial at the Whitney Museum of American Art, New York.

In 1990, in collaboration with Chicago architect John Vinci, Puryear designed a house and studio in upstate New York. He also received the Skowhegan Prize for sculpture.

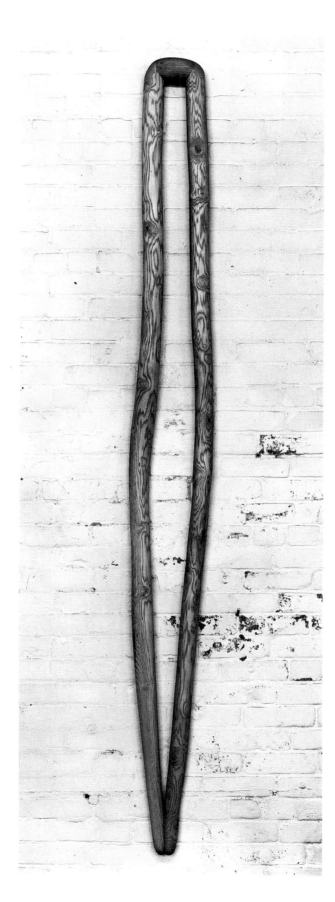

Martin Puryear, *Stripling*, 1976
Ash
85 × 10 in.
Truland Systems Corporation, Arlington,
Virginia

EXHIBITION HISTORY

Note: This chronology documents Martin Puryear's exhibited works as thoroughly as possible. We have been hampered somewhat by the unavailability of exhibition checklists in several instances, and by the fact that most of the work made prior to 1977 was destroyed that year in a fire. It should be pointed out that Puryear has often retitled and reconstituted sculptures from one exhibition to the next.

ONE-PERSON EXHIBITIONS

1968

Stockholm, Gröna Palletten Gallery, "Martin Puryear," May 18–May 30.

1972

Washington, D.C., Henri 2 Gallery, "Martin Puryear," January 8–February 4.
    1. *Hemlock Load, Oak Cast*, 1972
        Hemlock and oak
        50 × 48½ × 33 in.
    2. *Oak Wood Pile*, 1972
        Oak
        48 × 47 × 14 in.

Nashville, Fisk University, Carl van Vechten Gallery, "Pogue and Puryear," November 5–November 30. Exhibition brochure by Fred F. Bond.

1973

Washington, D.C., Henri 2 Gallery, "Martin Puryear," September 8–October 3.
    1. *Arkon Bwah*, 1973
        Willow and rope
        28 × 57 × 7 in.
    2. *Averted Polychrome*, 1971–72
        Poplar
        56 in. high
    3. *Bagged Flyseye Green*, 1972
        Osage orange and rope
        Toggles: 24 in. long
        Rope: 25 ft. long
    4. *Bound Cone*, 1973
        Oak and rope
        70 in. high
    5. *Crippled Cone*
        Oak and leather
    6. *Gravity's Sculpture*, 1971–72
        Poplar and concrete
        24 in. long
    7. *Hung-Over and Slung-Under*, 1972
        Calfskin
        20 in. high

8. *Narwhal-Pyramid*, 1971
   Pine
9. *Osage Beadwork*, 1973
   Osage orange and rope
   10 ft. long, dimensions variable
10. *Pedigree*, 1972
    Manila rope
    84 in. high × 10 ft. diameter
11. *Rope Chest*
    Manila rope
12. *Toggles*
    Osage orange
13. *Tope-Mill*, 1972
    Cherry and leather
    12 × 12 × 12 in.

1977

Washington, D.C., The Corcoran Gallery of Art,
"Martin Puryear," July 29–September 18.
   1. *Untitled*, 1975
      Oak and maple
      9 ft. 2 in. × 24 in. × 11 in.
   2. *Some Tales*, 1975–77
      Ash and yellow pine
      30 ft. long (approximately)
   3. *Bask*, 1976
      Staved dyed pine
      12 in. × 24 in. × 12 ft.
   4. *Cedar Lodge*, 1977
      Red cedar, fir, and rawhide
      18 ft. 2 in. high × 16 ft. 6 in. diameter

1978

Washington, D.C., Protetch-McIntosh Gallery, "Martin
Puryear," May 15–June 14.
   1. *Circumbent*, 1976
      Ash
      64 in. × 9 ft. 11¾ in. × 21 in.
   2. *Stripling*, 1976
      Ash
      85 × 10 in.
   3. *Untitled*, 1978
      African blackwood and vine
      15⅞ in. long
   4. *Untitled*, 1978
      Hickory and Alaskan yellow cedar
      60 × 78 × 1 in.
   5. *Untitled*, 1978
      Maple, Osage orange, and brass studs
      89 × 49½ × 9 in.
   6. *Untitled*, 1978
      Osage orange, yellow pine, and ash
      67 in. high × 14 in. diameter

1979

Washington, D.C., Protetch-McIntosh Gallery, "Martin
Puryear," November 20–December 15.
   1. *Blue Blood*, 1979
      Painted pine and red cedar
      66 × 66 × 2 in.
   2. *Na*, 1979 (as "*Untitled*")
      Painted pine
      62 × 63 × 6 in.
   3. *Nexus*, 1979
      Pine, maple, and gesso
      45 × 45 × 1½ in.
   4. *Noatak*, 1979
      Painted pine
      73¾ × 73¾ × 2¾ in.
   5. *Own*, 1979
      Painted basswood
      47¼ × 47¼ × 2¼ in.
   6. *Primavera*, 1979
      Painted pine and maple
      64¾ × 64 × 2 in.
   7. *Three Rings*, 1979
      Hickory sapling and ebony
      40¾ × 38¼ × 3¼ in.

1980

Chicago, Museum of Contemporary Art, "Options 2,"
February 1–March 11. Exhibition brochure by Judith
Russi Kirshner.
   1. *Equation for Jim Beckwourth*, 1980
      Pitch pine, oak, vines, rawhide, earth,
      and grass
      Dimensions variable

Chicago, Young Hoffman Gallery, "Martin Puryear,"
May 2–May 31.
   1. *Self*, 1978
      Painted red cedar and mahogany
      69 × 48 × 25 in.
   2. *Untitled*, 1979–80
      Pitch pine
      15½ × 23½ in.
   3. *Bower*, 1980
      Pine and Sitka spruce
      64 × 94¾ × 26⅝ in.
   4. *For Beckwourth*, 1980
      Earth, pitch pine, and oak
      40 × 34 × 34 in.
   5. *Reliquary*, 1980
      Gessoed pine
      12 × 47½ × 9 in.

Omaha, Nebraska, Joslyn Art Museum, "I-80 Series:
Martin Puryear," August 2–September 14. Exhibition
catalogue by Holliday T. Day.
   1. *Self*, 1978
      Painted red cedar and mahogany
      69 × 48 × 25 in.
   2. *Bower*, 1980
      Pine and Sitka spruce
      64 × 94¾ × 26⅝ in.
   3. *For Beckwourth*, 1980
      Earth, pitch pine, and oak
      40 × 34 × 34 in.
   4. *Pentagonal*, 1980
      Pine and Sitka spruce
      70 × 28½ × 28½ in.
   5. *Untitled*, 1980
      Osage orange
      27 × 12½ × 12½ in.

1981

Seattle, and/or, "Martin Puryear," May 21–June 13.
   1. *Where the Heart Is (Sleeping Mews)*, 1981
      Mixed-media installation
      Yurt: 18 ft. diameter

Dallas, Delahunty Gallery, "Martin Puryear," October
10–November 11.

1982

Washington, D.C., McIntosh/Drysdale Gallery, "Martin
Puryear," February 6–March 3.
   1. *Untitled*, 1979
      Painted ponderosa pine
      58 × 9⅜ in.
   2. *Azul-Azul*, 1981
      Painted basswood
      64 × 64 × 1¾ in.
   3. *Larx*, 1981
      Alaskan yellow cedar
      44 × 41½ × ⅞ in.
   4. *Minion*, 1981
      Painted ponderosa pine
      56 × 50 × 1⅞ in.
   5. *Stalk*, 1981
      Painted ponderosa pine and maple
      69 × 58 × 1⅞ in.
   6. *Yearn*, 1981
      Stained ponderosa pine
      56 × 56 × 1⅞ in.
   7. *Rapprochement*, 1982
      Painted ponderosa pine
      62 × 62 × 1⅞ in.

Installation of the exhibition "Martin Puryear: Ten Year Survey," University Gallery, University of Massachusetts, Amherst, 1984

Chicago, Young Hoffman Gallery, "Martin Puryear," May 21–July 6.

    1. *Red Yellow Blue*, 1981
        Painted ponderosa pine
        49½ × 61 × 8 in.

    2. *Cerulean*, 1982
        Painted pine
        63¾ × 63¼ × 1¾ in.

    3. *Kiruna*, 1982
        Painted gessoed pine
        59 × 57½ × 2¼ in.

    4. *Simple Gift*, 1982
        Pine, maple, and yellow cedar
        64 × 58¼ × 1¾ in.

    5. *Tango*, 1982
        Painted pine
        61 × 61½ × 2 in.

    6. *Thylacine*, 1982
        Tinted pine and yellow cedar
        59 × 56 × 33¼ in.

    7. *Untitled*, 1982
        Maple sapling, pear wood, and yellow cedar
        59 × 66 × 5 in.

1983

Chicago, Donald Young Gallery, "Martin Puryear," September 24–November 3.

    1. Maquettes for outdoor works

1984

Amherst, Massachusetts, University of Massachusetts, University Gallery, "Martin Puryear: Ten Year Survey," February 4–March 16. Exhibition catalogue by Hugh M. Davies and Helaine Posner.

    1. *Arkon Bwah*, 1973
        Willow and rope
        28 × 57 × 7 in.

    2. *Osage Beadwork*, 1973
        Osage orange and rope
        10 ft. long, dimensions variable

    3. *Untitled*, 1973
        Oak and steel wire
        21½ × 9¼ × 19¾ in.

    4. *Untitled*, 1975
        Dyed pine
        23 × 84 × 4½ in.

    5. *Bask*, 1976
        Staved dyed pine
        12 in. × 24 in. × 12 ft.

    6. *Stripling*, 1976
        Ash
        85 × 10 in.

    7. *Self*, 1978
        Painted red cedar and mahogany
        69 × 48 × 25 in.

8. *Some Lines for Jim Beckwourth*, 1978
   Twisted rawhide
   18 ft. (approximately)
9. *Untitled*, 1978
   African blackwood and vine
   15⁷⁄₈ in. long
10. *Untitled*, 1978
    Hickory and Alaskan yellow cedar
    60 × 78 × 1 in.
11. *Untitled*, 1978
    Osage orange, yellow pine, and ash
    67 in. high × 14 in. diameter
12. *Blue Blood*, 1979
    Painted pine and red cedar
    66 × 66 × 2 in.
13. *Bower*, 1980
    Pine and Sitka spruce
    64 × 94³⁄₄ × 26⁵⁄₈ in.
14. *For Beckwourth*, 1980
    Earth, pitch pine, and oak
    40 × 34 × 34 in.
15. *Reliquary*, 1980
    Gessoed pine
    12 × 47¹⁄₂ × 9 in.
16. *Big and Little Same*, 1981
    Ponderosa pine, painted pine, and
    unpainted pear wood
    61 × 62 × 2³⁄₄ in.
17. *Dream of Pairing*, 1981
    Painted pine
    51¹⁄₂ × 54¹⁄₂ × 2 in.
18. *Cerulean*, 1982
    Painted pine
    63³⁄₄ × 63¹⁄₄ × 1³⁄₄ in.
19. *Tango*, 1982
    Painted pine
    61 × 61¹⁄₂ × 2 in.
20. *Untitled*, 1982
    Bent maple sapling, pear wood, and
    yellow cedar
    59 × 66 × 5 in.

Note: also traveled to Pittsfield, Massachusetts, The Berkshire Museum, April 7–May 27; Boston, Museum of the National Center of Afro-American Artists, June 10–July 15; New York, The New Museum of Contemporary Art, July 28–September 9; La Jolla, California, The La Jolla Museum of Contemporary Art, October 13–December 9.

1985

Los Angeles, Margo Leavin Gallery, "Martin Puryear," January 12–February 16.
   1. *Boy's Toys #1*, 1984
      Yellow cedar, gourd, and wire
      13¹⁄₂ × 72⁷⁄₈ × 4¹⁄₂ in.
   2. *Boy's Toys #2*, 1984
      Sitka spruce, yellow cedar, and pear wood
      66⁵⁄₈ × 13¹⁄₄ × 6⁵⁄₈ in.
   3. *Boy's Toys #3*, 1984
      Painted pine
      16 × 62 × 8 in.
   4. *Boy's Toys #4*, 1984
      Gourd and copper
      52¹⁄₂ × 22¹⁄₄ × 6 in.
   5. *Boy's Toys #5*, 1984
      Painted pine
      57¹⁄₂ × 5 × 9 in.
   6. *Boy's Toys #6*, 1984
      Gourd, copper, and pear wood
      53³⁄₄ × 4¹⁄₂ × 4 in.
   7. *Boy's Toys #7*, 1984
      Yellow cedar
      43⁷⁄₈ × 5¹⁄₄ × 5¹⁄₄ in.
   8. *Boy's Toys #8*, 1984
      Steel pipe and red cedar
      22¹⁄₂ × 5¹⁄₄ × 7³⁄₄ in.
   9. *Boy's Toys #9*, 1984
      Red cedar and aluminum paint
      48³⁄₄ × 9³⁄₈ × 14 in.
   10. *Boy's Toys #10*, 1984
       Painted basswood and pine
       42 × 5³⁄₄ in. diameter
   11. *Boy's Toys #11*, 1984
       Calabash, copper, and wood
       51¹⁄₄ × 9¹⁄₄ in. diameter
   12. *Boy's Toys #12*, 1984
       Yellow cedar, basswood, and western
       red cedar
       32¹⁄₂ × 6¹⁄₄ × 6¹⁄₂ in.
   13. *Boy's Toys #13*, 1984
       Painted wood
       29 × 7³⁄₄ × 10¹⁄₈ in.
   14. *Keeper*, 1984
       Pine and steel wire
       100 × 34 × 38 in.
   15. *Lurk*, 1984
       Painted pine
       21³⁄₄ × 61¹⁄₄ × 7¹⁄₄ in.
   16. *Mus*, 1984
       Painted Sitka spruce, red cedar, and
       wire mesh
       44 × 26 in. diameter

   17. *Night and Day*, 1984
       Painted pine and wire
       83¹⁄₄ in. × 10 ft. × 6 in.
   18. *Seer*, 1984
       Painted pine and wire
       78 × 52¹⁄₂ × 45 in.
   19. *Vault*, 1984
       Douglas fir, pine, hemlock, wire mesh,
       and tar
       66 × 97 × 48 in.
   20. *Cask Cascade*, 1985
       Painted red cedar
       61³⁄₄ × 59¹⁄₂ × 30¹⁄₄ in.
   21. *Rogue Bull*, 1985
       Painted pine
       19 × 54¹⁄₄ × 5 in.

Berkeley, California, University Art Museum, "Martin Puryear: Matrix/Berkeley 86," July 31–September 22. Exhibition brochure by Constance Lewallen.
   1. *Nexus*, 1979
      Pine, maple, and gesso
      45 × 45 × 1¹⁄₂ in.
   2. *Boy's Toys #1*, 1984
      Yellow cedar, gourd, and wire
      13¹⁄₂ × 72⁷⁄₈ × 4¹⁄₂ in.
   3. *Boy's Toys #2*, 1984
      Sitka spruce, yellow cedar, and pear wood
      66⁵⁄₈ × 13¹⁄₄ × 6⁵⁄₈ in.
   4. *Boy's Toys #4*, 1984
      Gourd and copper
      52¹⁄₂ × 22¹⁄₄ × 6 in.
   5. *Boy's Toys #6*, 1984
      Gourd, copper, and pear wood
      53³⁄₄ × 4¹⁄₂ × 4 in.
   6. *Boy's Toys #8*, 1984
      Steel pipe and red cedar
      22¹⁄₂ × 5¹⁄₄ × 7³⁄₄ in.
   7. *Boy's Toys #9*, 1984
      Red cedar and aluminum paint
      48³⁄₄ × 9³⁄₈ × 14 in.
   8. *Boy's Toys #10*, 1984
      Painted basswood and pine
      42 × 5³⁄₄ in. diameter
   9. *Boy's Toys #12*, 1984
      Yellow cedar, basswood, and western
      red cedar
      32¹⁄₂ × 6¹⁄₄ × 6¹⁄₂ in.
   10. *Lurk*, 1984
       Painted pine
       21³⁄₄ × 61¹⁄₄ × 7¹⁄₄ in.
   11. *Cask Cascade*, 1985
       Painted red cedar
       61³⁄₄ × 59¹⁄₂ × 30¹⁄₄ in.

Martin Puryear, *Bask*, 1976
Staved dyed pine
12 in. × 12 ft. 2¾ in. × 24 in.
Solomon R. Guggenheim Museum, New
York, Exxon Corporation Purchase Award

Chicago, Donald Young Gallery, "Martin Puryear,"
October 11 – November 9.
    1. *Amulet*, 1985
        Pine and cypress
        63 × 62 × 8 in.
    2. *Endgame*, 1985
        Painted pine
        65 × 66 × 5 in.
    3. *In Winter Burrows*, 1985
        Tinted pine
        74 in. × 10 ft. 7 in. × 1¾ in.
    4. *Old Mole*, 1985
        Red cedar
        61 × 61 × 32 in.

    5. *Sanctum*, 1985
        Pine, wire mesh, and tar
        76 in. × 9 ft. 1 in. × 87 in.
    6. *The Spell*, 1985
        Pine, cedar, and steel
        56 × 84 × 65 in.
    7. *Untitled*, 1985
        Painted pine, steel mesh, and Kozo paper
        99 × 60 × 10 in.
    8. *Untitled*, 1985
        Wire mesh, cedar, and tar
        68 × 20 × 20 in.

1987

Chicago, Chicago Public Library Cultural Center, "Martin Puryear: Public and Personal," February 7–April 4. Exhibition catalogue by Deven K. Golden.

1. *Self*, 1978
   Painted red cedar and mahogany
   69 × 48 × 25 in.
2. *Bower*, 1980
   Pine and Sitka spruce
   64 × 94¾ × 26⅝ in.
3. *For Beckwourth*, 1980
   Earth, pitch pine, and oak
   40 × 34 × 34 in.
4. Proposal Model for *Knoll* (detail: bench), 1981
   Pine
   2 × 9 × 3 in.
5. Proposal Model for *Pavilion-in-the-Trees*, 1981
   Pressure-treated wood
   16 × 38½ × 11 in.
6. *Where the Heart Is (Sleeping Mews)*, 1981
   Mixed-media installation
   Yurt: 18 ft. diameter
7. *Chair*, 1982
   Bronze
   25¼ × 25¼ × 15 in.
8. *Sanctuary*, 1982
   Pine, maple, and cherry
   10 ft. 6 in. × 24 in. × 18 in.
9. *Lurk*, 1984
   Painted pine
   21¾ × 61¼ × 7¼ in.
10. *Mus*, 1984
    Painted Sitka spruce, red cedar, and wire mesh
    44 × 26 in. diameter
11. Proposal Model for *York College*, 1984
    Mixed-media
    18 × 28½ × 8¾ in.
12. *Seer*, 1984
    Painted pine and wire
    78 × 52½ × 45 in.
13. *Vault*, 1984
    Douglas fir, pine, hemlock, wire mesh, and tar
    66 × 97 × 48 in.
14. Model for *Shrine*, 1985
    Wood and wire mesh
    10¼ × 8½ × 9½ in.
15. Proposal Model for *Stone Bow*, 1985
    Painted wood
    9½ × 36 × 18 in.
16. *Untitled*, 1985
    Painted pine, steel mesh, and Kozo paper
    99 × 60 × 10 in.
17. *Untitled*, 1985
    Wire mesh, cedar, and tar
    68 × 20 × 20 in.
18. Drawing for *Chevy Chase Garden Plaza* (detail: gazebo), 1985–86
    Graphite on paper
    29 × 23 in.
19. Proposal Model for *Chevy Chase Garden Plaza* (detail: fountain), 1985–86
    Wood
    10 × 12¾ × 12¾ in.
20. Proposal Model for *Chevy Chase Garden Plaza* (detail: gazebo), 1985–86
    Wood
    6 × 7 × 6 in.

Pittsburgh, Carnegie Mellon University, Hewlett Art Gallery, "Martin Puryear: Sculpture and Works on Paper," April 12–May 30. Exhibition brochure by Elaine King.

1. Drawing for *Self*, 1978
   Pencil on tracing paper
   11½ × 8½ in.
2. *Self*, 1978
   Painted red cedar and mahogany
   69 × 48 × 25 in.
3. *Bower*, 1980
   Pine and Sitka spruce
   64 × 94¾ × 26⅝ in.
4. *For Beckwourth*, 1980
   Earth, pitch pine, and oak
   40 × 34 × 34 in.
5. *Thylacine*, 1982
   Tinted pine and yellow cedar
   59 × 56 × 3¼ in.
6. *Untitled*, 1982
   Maple sapling, pear wood, and yellow cedar
   59 × 66 × 5 in.
7. *Lurk*, 1984
   Painted pine
   21¾ × 61¼ × 7¼ in.
8. *Mus*, 1984
   Painted Sitka spruce, red cedar, and wire mesh
   44 × 26 in. diameter
9. *Vault*, 1984
   Douglas fir, pine, hemlock, wire mesh, and tar
   66 × 97 × 48 in.
10. *Untitled*, 1985
    Wire mesh, cedar, and tar
    68 × 20 × 20 in.
11. Etchings/Aquatints (7), 1966–68
12. Working Drawings (10), 1977–87

Chicago, Donald Young Gallery, "Martin Puryear," September 11–October 17.

1. *Untitled*, 1982
   Maple sapling, pear wood, and yellow cedar
   59 × 66 × 5 in.
2. *Maroon*, 1987 (as "*Untitled*," preliminary version)
   Steel mesh, tar, pine, yellow poplar, jute cord, and reed
   76 in. × 10 ft. × 30 ft. 6 in.
3. *To Transcend*, 1987
   Stained Honduras mahogany and poplar
   9 ft. 7½ in. × 7 ft. 6 in. × 13 ft.

New York, David McKee Gallery, "Martin Puryear: Stereotypes and Decoys," November 6–December 12.

1. *Empire's Lurch*, 1987
   Painted ponderosa pine
   75 × 48 × 25¼ in.
2. *From Somewhere Near the Equator*, 1987
   Honduras mahogany and gourd
   43 × 34 × 33 in.
3. *Sharp and Flat*, 1987
   Ponderosa pine
   64½ × 80 × 30 in.
4. *Timber's Turn*, 1987
   Honduras mahogany, red cedar, and Douglas fir
   87 × 61 × 48 in.
5. *Untitled*, 1987
   Tar, steel mesh, pine, and Douglas fir
   68 × 78 × 35 in.
6. *Verge*, 1987
   Red cedar and pine
   67½ × 86 × 47 in.

1988

Washington, D.C., McIntosh/Drysdale Gallery, "Martin Puryear: New Wall Sculpture," March 11–April 2.

1. *Untitled*, 1987
   Red cedar and pine
   9 ft. 5 in. × 22 in. × 17 in.
2. *The Cut*, 1988
   Red cedar and pine
   11 ft. 10 in. × 21 in. × 17 in.
3. *Divide*, 1988
   Red cedar and pine
   8 ft. 10 in. × 13 in. × 11 in.
4. *Generation*, 1988
   Painted red cedar and gourd
   8 ft. 5 in. × 43 in. × 20 in.
5. *Pride's Cross*, 1988
   Red cedar and poplar
   9 ft. 9 in. × 48 in. × 11¼ in.

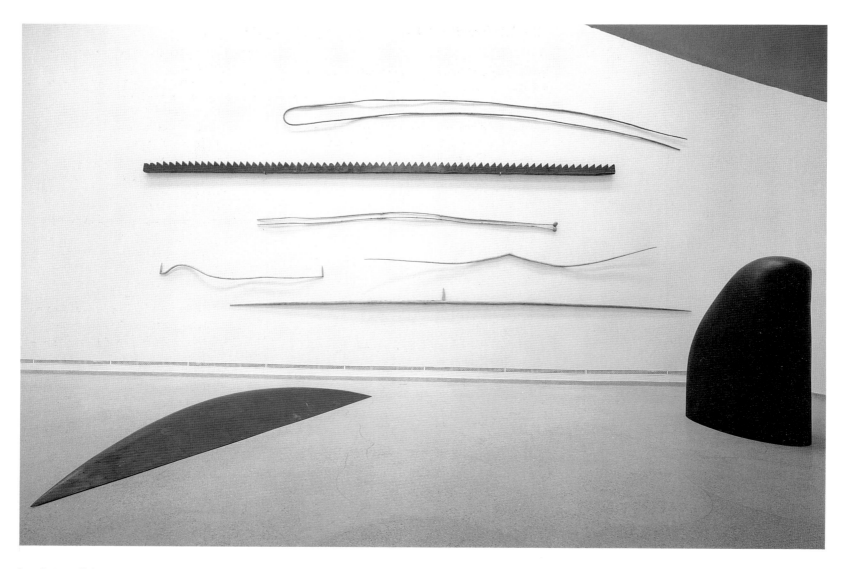

Installation of Martin Puryear sculpture in "Young American Artists, 1978 Exxon National Exhibition," Solomon R. Guggenheim Museum, New York, 1978

1988–89

Brooklyn, The Brooklyn Museum, "Martin Puryear," November 18, 1988–February 13, 1989.

1. *Desire*, 1981
   Pine, red cedar, poplar, and Sitka spruce
   16 ft. × 16 ft. × 31 ft. 10 in.
2. *Maroon*, 1987–88
   Steel mesh, tar, pine, and yellow poplar
   76 in. × 10 ft. × 78 in.

1989

Los Angeles, Margo Leavin Gallery, "Martin Puryear," April 15–May 20.

1. *Lever #1*, 1988–89 (as "*Lever*")
   Red cedar
   14 ft. 1 in. × 11 ft. 2 in. × 18 in.

2. *Lever #2*, 1988–89 (as "*Untitled*")
   Rattan, ponderosa pine, ash, and cypress
   71 in. × 24 ft. 5 in. × 55 in.
3. *Don-jon*, 1989 (as "*Untitled*")
   Painted ponderosa pine
   81¼ × 49 × 5¼ in.
4. *Lever #3*, 1989 (as "*Untitled*")
   Painted ponderosa pine
   84½ in. × 13 ft. 6 in. × 13 in.
5. *Lever #4*, 1989 (as "*Untitled*")
   Painted red cedar
   96 × 81 × 43 in.

São Paulo, "20th International São Paulo Bienal," October 14–December 10. Exhibition catalogue by Kellie Jones.

    I. *Rawhide Cone*, 1974 (second version, 1980; original destroyed in 1977)
        Rawhide
        51 × 63 × 32 in.

    2. *For Beckwourth*, 1980
        Earth, pitch pine, and oak
        40 × 34 × 34 in.

    3. *Untitled*, 1987
        Tar, steel mesh, pine, and Douglas fir
        68 × 78 × 35 in.

    4. *Maroon*, 1987–88
        Steel mesh, tar, pine, and yellow poplar
        76 in. × 10 ft. × 78 in.

    5. *Lever #1*, 1988–89 (as "*Lever*")
        Red cedar
        14 ft. 1 in. × 11 ft. 2 in. × 18 in.

    6. *Lever #2*, 1988–89 (as "*Untitled*")
        Rattan, ponderosa pine, ash, and cypress
        71 in. × 24 ft. 5 in. × 55 in.

    7. *The Charm of Subsistence*, 1989
        Rattan and gumwood
        85 × 66½ × 9½ in.

    8. *Lever #4*, 1989 (as "*Untitled*")
        Painted red cedar
        96 × 81 × 43 in.

1990

Boston, Museum of Fine Arts, "Connections: Martin Puryear," March 17–July 8. Exhibition brochure by Vishakha N. Desai and Kathy Halbreich.

    I. *On the Tundra*, 1981
        Cast iron
        19 × 9 × 11 in.

    2. *Where the Heart Is (Sleeping Mews)*, 1981
        Mixed-media installation
        Yurt: 18 ft. diameter

    3. *Untitled*, 1987
        Bronze
        16¾ × 24¼ × 8 in. (approximately)

    4. *Untitled*, 1989
        Curly maple
        16¾ × 24¼ × 8 in.

    5. Bronze Falcons (2)

    6. Glass Falcons (10)

    7. Wood Falcons (30)

GROUP EXHIBITIONS

1962

Washington, D.C., Adams-Morgan Gallery, "Puryear, Raymond, Termini."

1963

Baltimore, The Baltimore Museum of Art, "Maryland Regional Exhibition," March 10–April 7. Exhibition brochure by Charles Parkhurst.

    I. *Bull*, 1963
        Woodcut
    2. *Tree*, 1963
        Oil on canvas

1965

Freetown, Sierra Leone, United States Information Service Gallery, "Group Exhibition."

1967

Stockholm, Swedish Royal Academy of Art, "Annual Exhibition."

Stockholm, Liljevalchs Konstall, "Stockholm Biennial Exhibition."

1968

Stockholm, Swedish Royal Academy of Art, "Annual Exhibition," February 16–March 17.

1969

Washington, D.C., Lunn Gallery, "Group Exhibition."

1971

Madison, Wisconsin, University of Wisconsin Gallery, "Prints and Paintings by Black Artists."

1973

Washington, D.C., American Institute of Architects Headquarters, Octagon House.

1974

College Park, Maryland, University of Maryland Art Gallery, "New Talent at Maryland: Demonte, Puryear, Richer, Samuels, Willis," October 1–October 26.

Washington, D.C., National Collection of Fine Arts.

    I. *Oak Wood Pile*, 1972
        Oak
        48 × 47 × 14 in.
    2. *Osage Beadwork*, 1973
        Osage orange and rope
        10 ft. long, dimensions variable

1977

University Park, Pennsylvania, The Pennsylvania State University Museum of Art, "The Material Dominant: Some Current Artists and Their Media," January 29–March 27. Exhibition brochure.

    I. *Untitled*, 1976
        Oak and steel wire
        18½ × 9 × 22 in.

Lewiston, New York, Artpark, "The Program in the Visual Arts," August 4–September 11. Exhibition catalogue by Nancy Rosen.

    I. *Box and Pole*, 1977
        Canadian hemlock and southern yellow pine
        Box: 54 × 54 × 54 in.
        Pole: 100 ft. high

1978

New York, The Solomon R. Guggenheim Museum, "Young American Artists, 1978 Exxon National Exhibition," May 5–June 11. Exhibition catalogue by Linda Shearer.

    I. *Some Tales*, 1975–77
        Ash and yellow pine
        30 ft. long (approximately)
    2. *Bask*, 1976
        Staved dyed pine
        12 in. × 24 in. × 12 ft.
    3. *Self*, 1978
        Painted red cedar and mahogany
        69 × 48 × 25 in.

1978–79

New York, Whitney Museum of American Art, "The Presence of Nature," December 14, 1978–January 17, 1979. Exhibition brochure by Cindy Schwab.

    I. *Some Lines for Jim Beckwourth*, 1978
        Twisted rawhide
        18 ft. long (approximately)

1979

New York, Whitney Museum of American Art, "1979 Biennial Exhibition," February 6–April 8. Exhibition catalogue by John G. Hanhardt, Barbara Haskell, Richard Marshall, Mark Segal, and Patterson Sims.

    I. *M. Bastion Bouleversé*, 1978–79
        Hickory, Alaskan yellow cedar, and deerskin
        17 ft. × 18 ft. × 24 in.

New York, U.S. Customs House, "Customs and Culture," May 3–June 17.
> 1. *Her*, 1979
>> Red cedar and Douglas fir
>> 72 in. high
> 2. *She*, 1979
>> Red cedar and Douglas fir
>> 8 ft. 10 in. high

Bronx, Wave Hill, "Wave Hill, The Artist's View," May 15–October 28. Exhibition catalogue by Kirk Varnedoe.
> 1. *Equivalents*, 1979
>> Canadian hemlock
>> Box: 54 × 54 × 54 in.
>> Cone: 87½ × 75 × 75 in.

1980

Long Island City, New York, Institute for Art and Urban Resources, P.S. 1, "Afro-American Abstraction," February 17–April 6.
> 1. *Untitled*, 1978
>> Osage orange, yellow pine, and ash
>> 67 in. high × 14 in. diameter
> 2. *Own*, 1979
>> Painted basswood
>> 47¼ × 47¼ × 2¼ in.
> 3. *Three Rings*, 1979
>> Hickory sapling and ebony
>> 40¾ × 38¼ × 3¼ in.

Note: also traveled to Syracuse, New York, Everson Gallery, February 6–March 29, 1981.

Cincinnati, Contemporary Art Center, "Chicago, Chicago," October 3–November 9.
> 1. *Rawhide Cone*, 1974 (second version, 1980; original destroyed in 1977)
>> Rawhide
>> 51 × 63 × 32 in.
> 2. *Untitled*, 1975
>> Oak and maple
>> 110 × 24 × 11 in.
> 3. *Untitled*, 1980
>> Osage orange
>> 27 × 12½ × 12½ in.

Chicago, University of Illinois at Chicago, A. Montgomery Ward Gallery, "The Black Circle," February 4–February 29.
> 1. *Artpark Box and Pole*, 1977
>> Pencil on paper
>> 30 × 24 in.
> 2. *Artpark Box and Pole* (construction details), 1977
>> Pencil on paper
>> 30 × 24 in.

1981

New York, Whitney Museum of American Art, "1981 Biennial Exhibition," January 20–April 19. Exhibition catalogue by John G. Hanhardt, Barbara Haskell, Richard Marshall, and Patterson Sims.
> 1. *Na*, 1979
>> Painted pine
>> 62 × 63 × 6 in.
> 2. *Noatak*, 1979
>> Painted pine
>> 73¾ × 73¾ × 2¾ in.
> 3. *Bower*, 1980
>> Pine and Sitka spruce
>> 64 × 94¾ × 26⅝ in.

New York, School of Visual Arts, Visual Arts Museum, "Sculptural Density," March 30–April 24.
> 1. *On the Tundra*, 1981
>> Cast iron
>> 19 × 9 × 11 in.

Chicago, Museum of Contemporary Art, "Artists' Gardens and Parks," April 18–July 5. Exhibition brochure by Mary Jane Jacob and Lynne Warren.
> 1. *Proposal for Duncan Plaza*, 1980

Chicago, Chicago Public Library Cultural Center, "City Sculpture," July 18–September 5. Exhibition catalogue by Judith Russi Kirshner.
> 1. *Desire*, 1981
>> Pine, red cedar, poplar, and Sitka spruce
>> 16 ft. × 16 ft. × 31 ft. 10 in.

New York, Oscarsson Hood Gallery, "The New Spiritualism: Transcendent Images in Paintings and Sculpture," September 9–September 26. Exhibition catalogue by April Kingsley.
> 1. *Nexus*, 1979
>> Pine, maple, and gesso
>> 45 × 45 × 1½ in.

Note: also traveled to Storrs, Connecticut, University of Connecticut, Jorgensen Gallery, November 16–December 31; Burlington, Vermont, University of Vermont, Robert Hull Fleming Museum, February 4–March 28, 1982.

Bloomfield Hills, Michigan, Cranbrook Academy of Art, "Instruction Drawings," September 20–November 1. Exhibition catalogue by Michael Hall and Roy Slade.
> 1. *Plan for Cedar Lodge*, 1977
>> Pencil on vellum
>> 10 × 13 in.

1982

Providence, Rhode Island, Brown University, Bell Gallery of List Art Center, "Invitational Exhibition: Laurie Anderson, Farrell Brickhouse, Scott Burton, Denise Green, Wolfgang Laib, Joshua Neustein, Lucio Pozzi, Martin Puryear, Haim Steinbach," January 15–February 14. Exhibition catalogue by Roger Mayer.
> 1. *Rawhide Cone*, 1974 (second version, 1980; original destroyed in 1977)
>> Rawhide
>> 51 × 63 × 32 in.
> 2. *Some Lines for Jim Beckwourth*, 1978
>> Twisted rawhide
>> 18 ft. long (approximately)

Philadelphia, Pennsylvania Academy of Fine Arts, "FFA PFFAP: Form and Function, Proposals for Public Art in Philadelphia," February 19–April 18. Exhibition catalogue by Penny Belkin Bach.
> 1. Model for *Pavilion-in-the-Trees*, 1981
>> Wood
>> 17¼ × 11⅞ × 29³⁄₁₆ in.

Chicago, International Art Exposition, "Mayor Byrne's Mile of Sculpture," May 14–May 29.
> 1. *Desire*, 1981
>> Pine, red cedar, poplar, and Sitka spruce
>> 16 ft. × 16 ft. × 31 ft. 10 in.

Pittsburgh, Carnegie Mellon College of Fine Arts, Hewlett Gallery, "N.A.M.E. Gallery in Pittsburgh," June 1–June 30.

Chicago, The Art Institute of Chicago, "74th American Exhibition," June 12–August 1. Exhibition catalogue by Anne Rorimer.
> 1. *Believer*, 1977–82 (as "1980")
>> Poplar and pine
>> 23¼ × 23⅜ × 17⅜ in.
> 2. *Sanctuary*, 1982
>> Pine, maple, and cherry
>> 10 ft. 6 in. × 24 in. × 18 in.

Los Angeles, Los Angeles Municipal Art Gallery, "Afro-American Abstraction," July 1–August 30. Exhibition catalogue by April Kingsley for New York, The Art Museum Association.
> 1. *Rawhide Cone*, 1974 (second version, 1980; original destroyed in 1977)
>> Rawhide
>> 51 × 63 × 32 in.
> 2. *Stalk*, 1981
>> Painted ponderosa pine and maple
>> 69 × 58 × 1⅞ in.

Note: also traveled to Oakland, California, The Oakland Museum, November 13, 1982–January 2, 1983; Memphis, Brooks Memorial Art Gallery, February 10–March 24, 1983; South Bend, Indiana, The Art Center, September 4–October 16, 1983; Toledo, Ohio, The Toledo Museum of Art, January 22–February 26, 1984; Bellevue, Washington, Bellevue Art Museum, March 25–May 6, 1984; Austin, Texas, Laguna Gloria Art Museum, June 1–July 15, 1984; Jackson, Mississippi, Mississippi Museum of Art, September 14–November 4, 1984.

Los Angeles, Margo Leavin Gallery, "Works in Wood," July 10–September 11.
    1. *Big and Little Same*, 1981
        Ponderosa pine, painted pine, and
        unpainted pear wood
        61 × 62 × 2¾ in.

Richmond, Virginia, The Institute of Contemporary Art of the Virginia Museum, "American Abstraction Now," September 1–October 3. Exhibition catalogue by Julia Boyd.
    1. *Yearn*, 1981
        Stained ponderosa pine
        56 × 56 × 1⅞ in.
    2. *Untitled*, 1981–82
        Painted ponderosa pine
        58 in. diameter × 9⅜ in.

Martin Puryear, *Shrine*, 1985
Cypress and steel
10 ft. ½ in. × 10 ft. ½ in. × 9 ft.
Panza di Biumo Collection, Milan

1983

New York, Grace Borgenicht Gallery, "Invitational Exhibition," June 1–June 30.
1. *Cerulean*, 1982
   Painted pine
   63¾ × 63¼ × 1¾ in.
2. *Tango*, 1982
   Painted pine
   61 × 61½ × 2 in.

Cambridge, Massachusetts, Massachusetts Institute of Technology, Hayden Corridor Gallery, "Beyond the Monument, Documentation of Public Art Projects and Proposals," October 8–November 13. Exhibition brochure by Gary Garrels.
1. Proposal for *Pavilion-in-the-Trees*, 1983–84

1984

Chicago, Donald Young Gallery, "American Sculpture," April 28–July 28.
1. *Night and Day*, 1984
   Painted pine and wire
   83¼ in. × 10 ft. × 6 in.

New York, The Museum of Modern Art, "An International Survey of Recent Painting and Sculpture," May 17–August 19. Exhibition catalogue by Kynaston McShine.
1. *Believer*, 1977–82 (as "1980")
   Poplar and pine
   23¼ × 23⅜ × 17⅜ in.
2. *Sanctuary*, 1982
   Pine, maple, and cherry
   10 ft. 6 in. × 24 in. × 18 in.

Chicago, Rhona Hoffman Gallery, "Proposals & Projects: World Fairs, Waterfronts, Parks and Plazas," June 20–July 31.
1. Proposal for *Knoll for NOAA*, 1983

Los Angeles, Margo Leavin Gallery, "American Sculpture," July 17–September 15.
1. *Circumbent*, 1976
   Ash
   64 in. × 9 ft. 11 in. × 21 in.
2. *Nexus*, 1979
   Pine, maple, and gesso
   45 × 45 × 1½ in.

1984–85

New York, The Museum of Modern Art, "Primitivism in 20th Century Art: Affinity of the Tribal and the Modern," September 27, 1984–January 15, 1985. Exhibition catalogue by William S. Rubin and Kirk Varnedoe.
1. *Greed's Trophy*, 1984
   Hickory, ebony, rattan, and steel wire
   12 ft. 9 in. × 20 in. × 55 in.

1985

Hampton, Virginia, Hampton University, "Choosing: An Exhibit of Changing Modern Art and Art Criticism by Black Americans, 1925–1985," January 29–February 28. Exhibition catalogue by Jacqueline Fonvielle-Bontemps.
1. *Untitled*, 1973–74
   Oak and maple
   9 ft. 5 in. × 23 in. × 9 in.
2. *Rawhide Cone*, 1974 (second version, 1980; original destroyed in 1977)
   Rawhide
   51 × 63 × 32 in.
3. *For Beckwourth*, 1980
   Earth, pitch pine, and oak
   40 × 34 × 34 in.

Note: also traveled to Portsmouth, Virginia, Portsmouth Museum, February 1–March 31, 1986; Chicago, Chicago State University, May 1–May 31, 1986; Washington, D.C., Howard University, September 16–November 23, 1986.

Evanston, Illinois, Evanston Art Center, "Sculpture Overview 1985," February 7–March 17. Exhibition brochure by Stephen Luecking.
1. *Untitled*, 1975
   Oak and maple
   9 ft. 2 in. × 24 in. × 11 in.

Los Angeles, Los Angeles County Museum, Ahmanson Gallery, "The Artist as Social Designer: Aspects of Public Urban Art Today," February 7–March 17. Exhibition brochure by Maurice Tuchman.
1. Proposal for *Duncan Plaza*, 1980
2. Proposal for *Knoll for NOAA*, 1983

Chicago, "Chicago Sculpture International/Mile 4," May 9–June 9.
1. *Shrine*, 1985 (as "*Untitled*")
   Cypress and steel
   10 ft. ½ in. × 10 ft. ½ in. × 9 ft.

New York, The Solomon R. Guggenheim Museum, "Transformations in Sculpture: Four Decades in American and European Art," November 22, 1985–February 16, 1986. Exhibition catalogue by Diane Waldman.
1. *Bask*, 1976
   Staved dyed pine
   12 in. × 24 in. × 12 ft.
2. *Seer*, 1984
   Painted pine and wire
   78 × 52½ × 45 in.

Bologna, Galleria Communale d'Arte Moderna, "Anniottanta," July 4–September 30, 1985. Exhibition catalogue.
1. *Untitled*, 1973–74
   Oak and maple
   9 ft. 5 in. × 23 in. × 9 in.
2. *Rawhide Cone*, 1974 (second version, 1980; original destroyed in 1977)
   Rawhide
   51 × 63 × 32 in.
3. *Believer*, 1977–82 (as "1982")
   Poplar and pine
   23¼ × 23⅜ × 17⅜ in.

Note: This exhibition was also held at Imola, Chiostri di San Domenico; Ravenna, Chiostri della Loggetta Lombardesca e Biblioteca Classense; and Rimini, Castel Sismondo, Palazzina Mostre, Chiesa di Santa Maria ad Nives (Puryear's work at Bologna, Galleria Communale d'Arte Moderna).

1986

New York, Germans van Eck Gallery, "After Nature," February 1–February 28. Exhibition brochure by Steven Henry Madoff.
1. *Old Mole*, 1985
   Red cedar
   61 × 61 × 32 in.

Chicago, Donald Young Gallery, "Installations and Sculpture," May 2–May 31.
1. *Untitled*, 1986
   Poplar and painted pine
   83 × 64 × 2½ in.

Cambridge, Massachusetts, Massachusetts Institute of Technology, List Visual Arts Center, "Natural Forms and Forces: Abstract Images in American Sculpture," May 9–June 29. Exhibition catalogue by Katy Kline and Douglas Dreishpoon.
1. *For Beckwourth*, 1980
   Earth, pitch pine, and oak
   40 × 34 × 34 in.
2. *Cask Cascade*, 1985
   Painted red cedar
   61¾ × 59½ × 30¼ in.
3. *Endgame*, 1985
   Painted pine
   65 × 66 × 5 in.
4. *The Spell*, 1985
   Pine, cedar, and steel
   56 × 84 × 65 in.
5. *Two into One*, 1985
   Painted pine
   74 × 63 in.

Note: this exhibition was also held at Bank of Boston where works 2 and 4 were shown.

Kansas City, Missouri, Kansas City Art Institute, Charlotte Crosby Kemper Gallery, "Personal References," September 6–October 5. Exhibition brochure.

    1. *Circumbent*, 1976
        Ash
        64 in. × 9 ft. 11¾ in. × 21 in.
    2. *Self*, 1978
        Painted red cedar and mahogany
        69 × 48 × 25 in.
    3. *For Beckwourth*, 1980
        Earth, pitch pine, and oak
        40 × 34 × 34 in.
    4. *Amulet*, 1985
        Pine and cypress
        63 × 62 × 8 in.

1986–88

Los Angeles, The Museum of Contemporary Art, "Individuals: A Selected History of Contemporary Art 1945–1986," December 10, 1986–January 10, 1988. Exhibition catalogue by Julia Brown Turrell.

    1. *Greed's Trophy*, 1984
        Hickory, ebony, rattan, and steel wire
        12 ft. 9 in. × 20 in. × 55 in.
    2. *Keeper*, 1984
        Pine and steel wire
        8 ft. 4 in. × 34 in. × 38 in.
    3. *The Spell*, 1985
        Pine, cedar, and steel
        56 × 84 × 65 in.

1987

Buffalo, Albright-Knox Art Gallery, "Structure to Resemblance: Work by Eight American Sculptors," June 13–August 23. Exhibition catalogue by Michael Auping.

    1. *Sanctuary*, 1982
        Pine, maple, and cherry
        10 ft. 6 in. × 24 in. × 18 in.
    2. *Mus*, 1984
        Painted Sitka spruce, red cedar, and wire mesh
        44 × 26 in. diameter
    3. *Vault*, 1984
        Douglas fir, pine, hemlock, wire mesh, and tar
        66 × 97 × 48 in.
    4. *Endgame*, 1985
        Painted pine
        65 × 66 × 5 in.
    5. *Untitled*, 1985
        Wire mesh, cedar, and tar
        68 × 20 × 20 in.

New York, The Solomon R. Guggenheim Museum, "Emerging Artists 1978–1986: Selections from the Exxon Series," September 4–October 25. Exhibition catalogue by Diane Waldman.

    1. *Bask*, 1976
        Staved dyed pine
        12 in. × 24 in. × 12 ft..

1988

New York, R. C. Erpf Gallery, "Private Works for Public Spaces," February 19–March 19. Exhibition brochure by Jenny Dixon.

    1. *No Small Plans*, 1984–85
        Painted wood
        14½ × 17 × 10½ in.

New York, Whitney Museum of American Art, "Vital Signs: Organic Abstraction from the Permanent Collection," April 28–July 17. Exhibition catalogue by Lisa Phillips.

    1. *Sanctum*, 1985
        Pine, wire mesh, and tar
        76 in. × 9 ft. 1 in. × 87 in.

Milwaukee, The Milwaukee Art Museum, "1988: The World of Art Today," May 6–August 28.

    1. *Shrine*, 1985
        Cypress and steel
        10 ft. ½ in. × 10 ft. ½ in. × 9 ft.

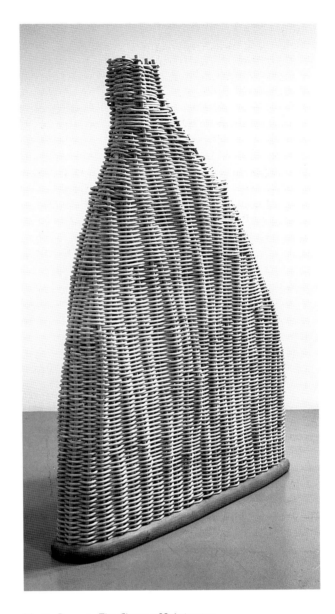

Martin Puryear, *The Charm of Subsistence*, 1989
Rattan and gumwood
85 × 66½ × 9½ in.
St. Louis Art Museum, Purchase: The Shoenberg Foundation, Inc., 105:1989

Minneapolis, Walker Art Center, "Sculpture Inside Outside," May 22–September 18. Exhibition catalogue by Martin Friedman, Donna Harkavy, and Peter W. Boswell.

1. *For Beckwourth*, 1980
   Earth, pitch pine, and oak
   40 × 34 × 34 in.
2. *Mus*, 1984
   Painted Sitka spruce, red cedar, and wire mesh
   44 × 26 in. diameter
3. *Two into One*, 1985
   Painted pine
   74 × 63 in.
4. *Noblesse O.*, 1987
   Red cedar and aluminum paint
   97 × 58 × 46 in.
5. *Timber's Turn*, 1987
   Honduras mahogany, red cedar, and Douglas fir
   87 × 61 × 48 in.
6. *To Transcend*, 1987
   Stained Honduras mahogany and poplar
   9 ft. 7½ in. × 90 in. × 13 ft.
7. *Untitled*, 1987
   Bronze
   18 × 14 × 6 in.
8. *Ampersand*, 1987–88
   Granite
   East column: 13 ft. 7 in. × 36 in. × 36 in.
   West column: 13 ft. 11 in. × 36 in. × 38 in.
9. *Generation*, 1988
   Painted red cedar and gourd
   8 ft. 5 in. × 43 in. × 20 in.

Note: numbers 1-7, 9 also traveled to Houston, The Museum of Fine Arts, December 10, 1988– March 3, 1989.

Aarau, Switzerland, Aargauer Kunsthaus, "Skulptur: Material+ Abstraktion: 2 × 5 Positionen," June 18– July 31. Exhibition catalogue by Corinne Diserens.

1. *Old Mole*, 1985
   Red cedar
   61 × 61 × 32 in.
2. *The Spell*, 1985
   Pine, cedar, and steel
   56 × 84 × 65 in.
3. *Timber's Turn*, 1987
   Honduras mahogany, red cedar, and Douglas fir
   87 × 61 × 48 in.

Note: also traveled to Lausanne, Switzerland, Musée Cantonal des Beaux-Arts, October 27– December 11; New York, City Gallery, January 5– February 10, 1989.

Saint Louis, The Saint Louis Art Museum, "New Sculpture/Six Artists," September 23–October 30. Exhibition brochure by Michael Edward Shapiro.

1. *The Cut*, 1988
   Red cedar and pine
   11 ft. 10 in. × 21 in. × 17 in.
2. *Pride's Cross*, 1988
   Red cedar and poplar
   9 ft. 9 in. × 48 in. × 11¼ in.
3. *Untitled*, 1988
   Red cedar and pine
   9 ft. 5 in. × 22 in. × 17 in.
4. *Lever #2*, 1988–89 (as "*Untitled*," earlier version)
   Rattan, ash, maple, and poplar
   10 ft. × 10 ft. 5 in. × 54 in.

Washington, D.C., The Corcoran Gallery of Art, "Edelson, Puryear, Scanga, Stackhouse," October 13– December 31. Exhibition brochure by Christopher French.

1. *Arkon Bwah*, 1973
   Willow and rope
   28 × 57 × 7 in.
2. *Stripling*, 1976
   Ash
   85 × 10 in.
3. *Some Lines for Jim Beckwourth*, 1978
   Twisted rawhide
   18 ft. long (approximately)
4. *On the Tundra*, 1981
   Cast iron
   19 × 9 × 11 in.

New York, Whitney Museum of American Art at Equitable Center, "Enclosing the Void: Eight Contemporary Sculptors," November 11, 1988–January 25, 1989. Exhibition catalogue by Susan Lubowsky.

1. *Untitled*, 1987
   Tar, steel mesh, pine, and Douglas fir
   68 × 78 × 35 in.

1989

Los Angeles, The California Afro-American Museum, "Introspectives: Contemporary Art by Americans and Brazilians of African Descent," February 11–September 30. Exhibition catalogue by Henry J. Drewel and David C. Driskell.

1. *On the Tundra*, 1981
   Cast iron
   19 × 9 × 11 in.
2. *Untitled*, 1982
   Cast bronze
   25¾ × 25½ × 14⅝ in.

Bronx, The Bronx Museum of the Arts, "Traditions and Transformations: Contemporary Afro-American Sculpture," February 21–May 27. Exhibition catalogue by Philip Verre.

1. *Rawhide Cone*, 1974 (second version, 1980; original destroyed in 1977)
   Rawhide
   51 × 63 × 32 in.
2. *The Spell*, 1985
   Pine, cedar, and steel
   56 × 84 × 65 in.

New York, Whitney Museum of American Art, "1989 Biennial Exhibition," April 27–July 9. Exhibition catalogue by Richard Armstrong, John G. Hanhardt, Richard Marshall, and Lisa Phillips.

1. *Verge*, 1987
   Red cedar and pine
   67½ × 86 × 47 in.
2. *The Cut*, 1988
   Red cedar and pine
   11 ft. 10 in. × 21 in. × 17 in.
3. *Pride's Cross*, 1988
   Red cedar and poplar
   9 ft. 9 in. × 48 in. × 11¼ in.

Chicago, Donald Young Gallery, "New Sculpture: Tony Cragg, Richard Deacon, Martin Puryear, Susana Solano," May 3–May 27.

1. *The Charm of Subsistence*, 1989
   Rattan and gumwood
   85 × 66½ × 9½ in.
2. *Untitled*, 1989
   Red cedar
   10 ft. 8 in. × 16¾ in. × 21 in.

New York, Whitney Museum of American Art, "Art in Place: Fifteen Years of Acquisitions," July 27– October 22. Exhibition catalogue by Tom Armstrong and Susan C. Larsen.

1. *Sanctum*, 1985
   Pine, wire mesh, and tar
   76 in. × 9 ft. 1 in. × 87 in.

1990

Belmont, California, College of Notre Dame, Wiegand Gallery, "Objects of Potential: Five American Sculptors from the Anderson Collection," February 6–March 30. Exhibition brochure by David Cateforis.

    1. *Untitled*, 1978
        Osage orange, yellow pine, and ash
        67 in. high × 14 in. diameter
    2. *Sharp and Flat*, 1987
        Ponderosa pine
        64½ × 80 × 30 in.
    3. *Lever #4*, 1989
        Painted red cedar
        96 × 81 × 43 in.

New York, The New Museum for Contemporary Art, "The Decade Show: Frameworks of Identity in the 1980s," May 12–August 19. Exhibition catalogue.

    1. *Untitled*, 1987
        Red cedar and pine
        9 ft. 5 in. × 22 in. × 17 in.

Note: this exhibition was also held at New York, Museum of Contemporary Hispanic Art, May 16–August 19; and New York, The Studio Museum of Harlem, May 18–August 19 (Puryear's work at The Studio Museum of Harlem).

Martin Puryear, *Lever #3*, 1989
Painted ponderosa pine
84½ in. × 13 ft. 6 in. × 13 in.
National Gallery of Art, Washington, D.C.,
Gift of the Collector's Committee,
1989.71.1

SITED, OUTDOOR, and PROPOSED WORKS

Martin Puryear, *Sentinel*, 1982
Mortared fieldstone
10 ft. 6 in. × 8 ft. 6 in. × 42 in.
Gettysburg College, Gettysburg,
Pennsylvania

1977

Lewiston, New York, Artpark
  1. *Box and Pole*, 1977
      Canadian hemlock and southern
      yellow pine
      Box: 54 × 54 × 54 in.
      Pole: 100 ft. high

1978

Warren, Michigan, Macomb Community College
  1. *Untitled*, 1978
      Hemlock
      10 × 10 × 10 ft.

1979

New York, U.S. Customs House
  1. *Her*, 1979
      Red cedar and Douglas fir
      72 in. high
  2. *She*, 1979
      Red cedar and Douglas fir
      8 ft. 10 in. high

Bronx, New York, Wave Hill
  1. *Equivalents*, 1979
      Canadian hemlock
      Box: 54 × 54 × 54 in.
      Cone: 87½ × 75 × 75 in.

1980

New Orleans, Duncan Plaza
  1. *Duncan Plaza Project*
      Concrete and plantings
      Unbuilt

1981

Seattle, National Oceanic and Atmospheric Administration, Western Regional Center
  1. *Knoll for NOAA*, 1981 (built 1983)
      Concrete and plantings
      Knoll: 45 ft. diameter × 54 in. high

Philadelphia, Cliveden Park
  1. *Pavilion-in-the-Trees*, 1981
      Pressure-treated wood
      Unbuilt

1982

Gettysburg, Pennsylvania, Gettysburg College
  1. *Sentinel*, 1982
      Mortared fieldstone
      10 ft. 6 in. × 8 ft. 6 in. × 42 in.

University Park, Illinois, Governors State University, The Nathan Manilow Sculpture Park
  1. *Bodark Arc*, 1982
      Wood, asphalt, and bronze
      392 ft. diameter

1985

Bethesda, Maryland, Chevy Chase Garden Park
  1. *Chevy Chase Garden Plaza*, 1985 (built 1990)
      Mixed-media
      Fountain: 8 ft. 6 in. × 12 ft. × 72 in.

Chicago, Chicago O'Hare Transit Line, River Road Station
  1. *River Road Ring*, 1985
      Honduras mahogany
      27 ft. 6 in. × 27 ft. 6 in. × 6 in.

Pittsburgh, Port Authority of Allegheny County, Penn Park Station
  1. *No Small Plans*, 1984–85
      Welded steel
      Unbuilt

Medford, Massachusetts, Tufts University
  1. *Stone Bow*, 1985
      Granite
      Unbuilt

1986

Jamaica, New York, The City University of New York, York College
  1. *Ark*, 1986
      Copper
      36 × 72 ft.

1988

Minneapolis, Walker Art Center, Minneapolis Sculpture Garden
  1. *Ampersand*, 1987–88
      Granite
      East column: 13 ft. 7 in. × 36 in. × 36 in.
      West column: 13 ft. 11 in. × 36 in. × 38 in.

SELECTED BIBLIOGRAPHY

"A Bienal Abre Em Crise: Von Schimdt Se Demite." *Jornal da Tarde*, October 16, 1989, p. 21.

"A Bienal Já Abre Com Vencedores." *Jornal da Tarde*, October 14, 1989, p. 4.

Aarau, Switzerland, Aargauer Kunsthaus. *Sculpture: Material and Abstraction: 2 x 5 Points of View*. Exhibition catalogue by Corinne Diserens. Aarau, 1985.

Aguilar, Nelson. "Puryear e Klein Atraem Visitante da 20a Bienal." *Folha de S. Paulo*, October 18, 1989, p. F12.

Allen, Terry Y. "The Unconventional Eye." *Amherst Magazine*, Summer 1990, pp. 14–17.

Amherst, Massachusetts, University of Massachusetts, University Gallery. *Martin Puryear*. Exhibition catalogue by Hugh M. Davies and Helaine Posner. Amherst, 1984.

Anderaos, Ricardo. "Obras de Stella Não Cabem No Espaço Reservado." *Folha de S. Paulo*, October 12, 1989, p. F5.

Arnason, H.K. *History of Modern Art, Third Edition*. New York: Harry N. Abrams, 1986.

Artner, Alan G. "Martin Puryear, Museum of Contemporary Art." *Chicago Tribune*, February 22, 1980, sec. 3, p. 13.

_____. "Martin Puryear." *Chicago Tribune*, June 25, 1982, sec. 3, p. 13.

_____. "N.Y.'s 'Primitive' Show a Modern Masterpiece." *Chicago Tribune*, November 4, 1984, sec. 13, pp. 13–14.

_____. "Jury to Select 'Mile 4' Winner." *Chicago Tribune*, May 23, 1985, sec. 5, p. B16.

_____. "Perfection is Hallmark of Puryear Sculpture." *Chicago Tribune*, October 25, 1985, sec. 7, pp. 51–52.

_____. "A Sculptor's 2 Sides; Martin Puryear on His Public and Private Art." *Chicago Tribune*, February 1, 1987, sec. 13, pp. 14–15.

_____. "Massive Work a Visual Odyssey." *Chicago Tribune*, September 17, 1987, sec. 5, p. 10.

_____. "Shaping Up." *Chicago Tribune*, October 1, 1989, sec. 13, p. 13.

_____. "Public Sculpture's Changing Face." *Chicago Tribune*, August 26, 1990, sec. 13, pp. 16–17.

Ashbery, John. "The Sculptures of Summer." *New York Magazine* 12, 29 (July 23, 1979), pp. 57–58.

_____. "Vision of the Olympics." *Newsweek* 51, 4 (January 24, 1983), p. 73.

"Awards." *Art in America* 77, 6 (June 1989), p. 206.

Baker, Kenneth. "Journal of the Puryear." *The Boston Phoenix*, July 10, 1984, sec. 3, pp. 5, 14.

Baltimore, The Baltimore Museum of Art. *Maryland Regional Exhibition*. Exhibition brochure by Charles Parkhurst. Baltimore, 1963.

Belik, Helio. "Representante dos EUA na Bienal Chega Sábado Para Estudar Espaço." *Folha de S. Paulo*, February 9, 1989, p. E1.

Belluzze, Ana Maria M. "As Possibilidades Espaciais da Bienal." *Jornal da Tarde*, November 6, 1989, p. 28.

Belmont, California, College of Notre Dame, Wiegand Gallery. *Objects of Potential: Five American Sculptors from the Anderson Collection*. Exhibition brochure by David Cateforis. Belmont, 1990.

Benevides, Daniel. "Constrüçoes de Puryear, Filtradas em Musseline." *Jornal da Tarde*, October 12, 1989, p. 20.

Berkeley, California, University Art Museum. *Martin Puryear: Matrix/Berkeley 86*. Exhibition brochure by Constance Lewallen. Berkeley, 1985.

Berkson, Bill. "Seattle Sites." *Art in America* 74, 7 (July 1986), pp. 68–82, 133, 135.

Berkowitz, Marc. "São Paulo Biennale: No Hidden Corners." *Artnews* 89, 2 (February 1990), p. 167.

Beuttenmuller, Alberto. "Richard Hamilton e Eventos Salvam a Bienal." *O Estado de S. Paulo*, October 15, 1989, p. 6.

_____. "A Bienal, Como Retrospectiva dos Ultimos 20 Anos." *O Estado de S. Paulo*, October 24, 1989, p. 3.

"Bienal Abre Hoje Sob Tensão." *Folha de S. Paulo*, October 14, 1989, p. 1.

Bloomfield Hills, Michigan, Cranbrook Academy of Art. *Instruction Drawings*. Exhibition catalogue by Michael Hall and Roy Slade. Bloomfield Hills, 1981.

Bois, Yve-Alain. "La Pensée Sauvage." *Art in America* 73, 4 (April 1985), pp. 178–98.

Bologna, Galleria Comunale d'Arte Moderna. *Anniottanta*. Exhibition catalogue. Bologna, 1985.

Bonesteel, Michael. "Summer Solstice for Chicago Art." *New Art Examiner* 9, 1 (October 1981), pp. 6–7.

Bonetti, David. "Back to Natural: Sculpture Takes on the World." *The Boston Phoenix*, June 3, 1986, pp. 4–5.

Boston, Museum of Fine Arts. *Connections: Martin Puryear*. Exhibition brochure by Vishakha N. Desai and Kathy Halbreich. Boston, 1990.

Bourdon, David. "Martin Puryear at Henri 2." *Art in America* 62, 1 (January/February 1974), p. 110.

_____. "Washington Revisited." *Art in America* 66, 4 (July/August 1978), pp. 95–99.

Brenson, Michael. "Sculptors Find New Ways with Wood." *The New York Times*, December 2, 1982, sec. 2, pp. 29, 32.

_____. "Sculpture: Puryear Postminimalism." *The New York Times*, August 10, 1984, p. C24.

_____. "Art: The Human Form in Work of 12 Sculptors." *The New York Times*, February 1, 1985, p. C24.

_____. "How Sculpture Freed Itself from the Past." *The New York Times*, December 15, 1985, sec. 2, p. 39.

_____. "Sculpture Breaks the Mold of Minimalism." *The New York Times*, November 23, 1986, sec. 2, pp. 1, 33.

_____. "Maverick Sculptor Makes Good." *The New York Times*, November 1, 1987, sec. 5, pp. 84, 88, 90, 92–93.

_____. "Shaping the Dialogue of Mind and Matter." *The New York Times*, November 22, 1987, sec. 2, pp. 39–42.

_____. "Works for Urban College Raise Hard Questions." *The New York Times*, April 8, 1988, p. C32.

_____. "'Enclosing the Void': Sculptural Interiors with the Lightness of Being." *The New York Times*, November 18, 1988, p. C22.

_____. "Sculptor to Represent U.S. at the São Paulo Biennale." *The New York Times*, November 22, 1988, p. C19.

_____. "Doors of Art Opening." *The New York Times*, October 16, 1989, pp. B11, 14.

_____. "A Sculptor's Struggle to Fuse Culture and Art." *The New York Times*, October 29, 1989, pp. H37, 39.

_____. "Puryear: a Arte Desafiando Limites." *Jornal da Tarde*, October 31, 1989, p. 18.

Bright, Deborah. "Bruce Nauman, Martin Puryear." *New Art Examiner* 11, 3 (December 1983), p. 17.

Bronx, Wave Hill. *Wave Hill, The Artist's View*. Exhibition catalogue by Kirk Varnedoe. Bronx, 1979.

Bronx, The Bronx Museum of the Arts. *Traditions and Transformations: Contemporary Afro-American Sculpture*. Exhibition catalogue by Philip Verre. Bronx, 1989.

Brown, Mark. "Grants Give 'Geniuses' Freedom." *Chicago Sun-Times*, July 18, 1989, p. 7.

Buffalo, Albright-Knox Art Gallery. *Structure to Resemblance: Work by Eight American Sculptors*. Exhibition catalogue by Michael Auping. Buffalo, 1987.

"Caderno 2." *O Estado de S. Paulo*, October 14, 1989, p. 1.

Calo, Carole Gold. "Martin Puryear: Private Objects, Evocative Visions." *Arts* 62, 6 (February 1988), pp. 90–93.

_____. "Martin Puryear, David McKee Gallery." *New Art Examiner* 15, 6 (February 1988), p. 65.

Cambridge, Massachusetts, Massachusetts Institute of Technology, Hayden Corridor Gallery. *Beyond the Monument: Documentation of Public Art Projects and Proposals*. Exhibition brochure by Gary Garrels. Cambridge, 1983.

Cambridge, Massachusetts, Massachusetts Institute of Technology, List Visual Arts Center. *Natural Forms and Forces: Abstract Images in American Sculpture*. Exhibition catalogue by Katy Kline and Douglas Dreishpoon. Cambridge, 1986.

Catlin, Roger. "Joslyn Opens Small Show." *Sunday World-Herald Magazine* (Omaha), August 24, 1980, Entertainment sec., p. 27.

Chicago, Chicago Public Library Cultural Center. *Martin Puryear: Public and Personal*. Exhibition catalogue by Deven K. Golden. Essays by Patricia Fuller and Judith Russi Kirshner. Chicago, 1987.

_____. *City Sculpture*. Exhibition brochure by Judith Russi Kirshner. Chicago, 1981.

Chicago, Museum of Contemporary Art. *Options 2: Martin Puryear*. Exhibition brochure by Judith Russi Kirshner. Chicago, 1980.

_____. *Artists' Parks and Gardens*. Exhibition brochure by Mary Jane Jacob and Lynne Warren. Chicago, 1981.

"Chicago Sculptor Puryear Wins Top Prize in Art Show." *Chicago Sun-Times*, October 15, 1989, p. 8.

"Chicago Sculptor Wins Top Prize in São Paulo." *Chicago Tribune*, October 15, 1989, sec. 1, p. 5.

Chicago, The Art Institute of Chicago. *74th American Exhibition*. Exhibition catalogue by Anne Rorimer. Chicago, 1982.

Clark, Vicky A. "Primal Forms." *Dialogue*, September/October 1987, p. 52.

Colker, Ed. "Present Concerns in Studio Teaching: Artists Statements." *Art Journal* 42, 1 (Spring 1982), p. 36.

Comodo, Roberto. "A Festa da Nova Forma." *Jornal do Brasil*, October 14, 1989, p. 1.

Conn, Sandra. "Move to State Street Boosts Mile of Sculpture's Image." *Crain's Chicago Business* 8, 11 (March 18, 1985), p. 16.

Cotter, Holland. "A Bland Biennial." *Art in America* 77, 9 (September 1989), pp. 81–87.

Crary, Jonathan. "Martin Puryear's Sculpture." *Artforum* 18, 2 (October 1979), pp. 28–31.

Dale, Steve. "A New Look to State Street: Sculpture Invitational Debuts." *Chicago Tribune*, May 10, 1985, sec. 7, p. 4.

Danoff, I. Michael. "How the Sculptures Were Selected for State St. Exhibition." *Chicago Sun-Times*, May 5, 1985, p. 10.

Davis, Robert. "$355,000 Grant Lets Teacher Know She's Really Worth It." *Chicago Tribune*, July 18, 1989, sec. 1, pp. 1–2.

De Vuono, Frances. "The Decade Show." *Artnews* 89, 9 (November 1990), pp. 165–66.

Donohue, Marlena. "The Galleries." *Los Angeles Times*, April 21, 1989, sec. 6, p. 23.

Evanston, Illinois, Evanston Art Center. *Sculpture-Overview 1985.* Exhibition brochure by Stephen Luecking. Evanston, 1985.

Flam, Jack. "The View from the Cutting Edge." *The Wall Street Journal,* May 10, 1989, p. A16.

Fleming, Lee. "Martin Puryear, McIntosh-Drysdale Gallery." *The Washington Review* 7, 6 (April/May 1982), p. 28.

Forgey, Benjamin. "Martin Puryear." *Washington Evening Star,* September 19, 1973, n.pag.

_____. "Draftsmanship and Woodmanship." *Artnews* 77, 1 (January 1978), pp. 118–22.

_____. "Puryear's Circles: Subtle, Brooding Presence." *The Washington Star,* December 7, 1979, p. C3.

_____. "Craft Comes Full Circle to Art." *The Washington Post,* February 25, 1982, p. B7.

Francis, Paulo. "A Bienal de Von Schmidt." *Folha de S. Paulo,* October 22, 1989, p. D4.

Freire, Norma. "Roupa Suja se Lava Numa Bienal de Arte." *O Estado de S. Paulo,* October 17, 1989, p. 1.

Friedman, Martin. "Growing the Garden." *Design Quarterly* 141 (Fall 1988), cover, pp. 4–43.

Fucuta, Brenda. "Na Bienal Olhos Atentos Descobrema Arte de Ver Arte." *Jornal da Tarde,* October 27, 1989, pp. A10–11.

Galvao, Joao Candido. "Em Busca da Essencia." *Guia das Artes Internacional* 3, 13 (1990), pp. 49–51.

Gast, V. Dwight. "Martin Puryear: Sculpture as an Act of Faith." *The Journal of Art* 2, 1 (September/October 1989), pp. 6–7.

Giannini, Alessandro. "Bienal: Os Primeiros Nomes do Exterior." *Jornal da Tarde,* January 27, 1989, p. 22.

Glueck, Grace. "Artists of the Customs House." *The New York Times,* May 4, 1979, p. C21.

_____. "Serving the Environment." *The New York Times,* June 27, 1982, pp. H25–26.

Halim, Gisella. "Yes, Nós Temos Bienal." *Vogue Magazine,* October 1989, pp. 130–33.

Hampton, Virginia, Hampton University. *Choosing: An Exhibit of Changing Modern Art and Art Criticism by Black Americans, 1925–1985.* Exhibition catalogue by Jacqueline Fonvielle-Bontemps. Hampton, 1985.

Hanson, Henry. "Puryear's Poster." *Chicago Magazine* 32, 7 (July 1983), p. 13.

_____. "Martin Puryear Scores Big at Brazil Bienal." *Chicago Magazine* 39, 1 (January 1990), p. 20.

Harris, Stacy Paleologos, ed. *Insights/On Sights: Perspectives on Art in Public Places.* Washington, D.C.: Partners for Livable Places, 1984.

Hellman, Marla. "LJMCA & Puryear: What a Combination." *The UCSD Guardian,* November 8, 1984, p. 1.

Holland, Laura. "Martin Puryear: Sculpture, Berkshire Museum, Pittsfield." *Art New England* 5, 6 (May 1984), p. 12.

Horsfield, Kate, and Lyn Blumenthal, eds. *Profile: Martin Puryear.* Chicago: Video Data Bank, The School of The Art Institute of Chicago, 1977.

Hughes, Robert. "Going Back to Africa—as Visitors." *Time* 115, 13 (March 31, 1980), p. 72.

Hunsecker, J. J. "Naked City." *Spy Magazine,* April 1990, p. 48.

Huntington, Richard. "Albright-Knox Turns Good Idea into Fine Show." *The Buffalo News,* August 2, 1987, pp. G1, 5.

Jamaica, New York, Jamaica Arts Center. *Martin Puryear.* 20th International São Paulo Bienal 1989. Exhibition catalogue by Kellie Jones. Jamaica, 1989.

Joselit, David. "Lessons in Public Sculpture." *Art in America* 77, 12 (December 1989), pp. 131–35.

Kangas, Mathew. "Martin Puryear, and/or Gallery Seattle." *Vanguard* 10, 7 (September 1981), p. 42.

Kansas City, Missouri, Kansas City Art Institute. *Personal References: Raymond Saunders, Phyllis Bramson, Martin Puryear.* Exhibition brochure. Kansas City, 1986.

Kaufman, Jason Edward. "XXth São Paulo Bienal." *Art Papers* 14, 1 (January/February 1990), p. 69.

Kelley, Jeff. "Puryear's Sculpture Casts Spell." *Los Angeles Times,* October 29, 1984, sec. 6, pp. 1, 3.

Kimmelman, Michael. "Martin Puryear, The Brooklyn Museum." *The New York Times,* December 2, 1988, p. C24.

_____. "The Force of Conviction Stirred by the 80's." *The New York Times,* May 27, 1990, sec. 2, pp. 25, 30.

Kingsley, April. "The Shapes Arise." *The Village Voice* 24, 32 (July 30, 1979), p. 70.

_____. "Artpark and the Leisure Landscape." *Art Express* 2, 3 (May/June 1982), pp. 27–29.

_____. "Public Art." *Art Express* 2, 3 (May/June 1982), p. 13.

Kirshman, Cindy. "Earthworks Art Sways with Its Dimension." *Chicago Tribune,* April 3, 1987, sec. 7, p. 58.

Kirshner, Judith Russi. "Martin Puryear, Margo Leavin Gallery." *Artforum* 23, 10 (Summer 1985), p. 115.

Knight, Christopher. "Afro-American Abstraction: More Abstract than African." *Los Angeles Herald Examiner,* July 14, 1982, pp. D1, 6.

_____. "Sculptures with a Touch of Nature." *Los Angeles Herald Examiner,* May 12, 1989, p. D4.

Krainak, Paul. "Contraprimitivism and Martin Puryear." *Art Papers* 13, 2 (March/April 1989), pp. 39–40.

Lagnado, Lisette. "A Bienal Desmontada." *Guia das Artes Internacional* 4, 17 (1990), p. 97.

Lautman, Victoria. "Martin Puryear: Chicago Public Library Cultural Center." *Sculpture* 6, 4 (July/August 1987), pp. 28–29.

Lewis, Jo Ann. "Washington, D.C." *Artnews* 79, 3 (March 1980), p. 150.

Lewiston, New York, Artpark. *Artpark 1977: The Program in the Visual Arts*. Exhibition catalogue by Nancy Rosen. Lewiston, 1977.

Lima, Denise. "Torre de Babel Artística." *O Globo*, October 13, 1989, p. 1.

Los Angeles, The California Afro-American Museum. *Introspectives: Contemporary Art By Americans and Brazilians of African Descent*. Exhibition catalogue by Henry J. Drewel and David C. Driskell. Los Angeles, 1989.

Los Angeles, Los Angeles County Museum of Art, Ahmanson Gallery. *The Artist as Social Designer: Aspects of Public Urban Art Today*. Exhibition brochure by Maurice Tuchman. Los Angeles, 1985.

Los Angeles, Los Angeles Municipal Art Gallery. See New York, The Art Museum Association.

Los Angeles, The Museum of Contemporary Art. *Individuals: A Selected History of Contemporary Art 1945–1986*. Exhibition catalogue by Julia Brown Turrell. Los Angeles, 1986.

Luecking, Stephen. "Monumental Sculpture, Speaking the Language of Wood." *Fine Woodworking*, January/February 1985, pp. 66–69.

Madoff, Steven Henry. "Sculpture Unbound." *Artnews* 85, 9 (November 1986), pp. 103–09.

Mageste, Paula. "Bienal Abre Sem Estar Pronta." *Folha da Tarde*, October 14, 1989, p. 17.

Mammr, Lorenzo. "Um Ponto De Extase." *Galeria* 17 (1989), pp. 66–70.

Margarido, Orlando C. "Bienal Toda a Arte do Mundo em São Paulo." *Manchete Magazine*, November 4, 1989, pp. 70–77.

Margutti, Mario. "O Crescimento Organico da Obra." *Atualidades*, October 17, 1989, n.pag.

"Martin Puryear." *Jornal da Tarde*, October 14, 1989, p. 4.

McGill, Douglas C. "Art People." *The New York Times*, January 29, 1988, p. C26.

Menzies, Neal. "Unembellished Strength of Form." *Artweek* 16, 5 (February 2, 1985), p. 4.

Minneapolis, Walker Art Center. *Sculpture Inside Outside*. Exhibition catalogue by Martin Friedman, Donna Harkavy, and Peter W. Boswell. Minneapolis, 1988.

Morgan, Ann Lee. "Martin Puryear: Sculpture as Elemental Expression." *New Art Examiner* 14, 9 (May 1987), pp. 27–29.

Morgan, Robert C. "American Sculpture and the Search for a Referent." *Arts* 62, 3 (November 1987), pp. 20–23.

Morrison, Keith. "Questioning the Quality Canon." *New Art Examiner* 18, 2 (October 1990), pp. 24–27.

Moser, Charlotte. "Chicago: Martin Puryear at Donald Young." *Artnews* 85, 1 (January 1986), p. 116.

Muchnic, Suzanne. "The Abstract Shapes of Familiar Mysteries." *Los Angeles Times*, January 15, 1985, sec. 6, pp. 1, 4.

Nadelman, Cynthia. "Broken Premises: 'Primitivism' at MoMA." *Artnews* 85, 2 (February 1985), pp. 88–95.

Nashville, Fisk University, Carl van Vechten Gallery. *Pogue and Puryear*. Exhibition brochure by Fred F. Bond. Nashville, 1972.

Nemser, Mary Rebecca. "Flying High: Martin Puryear Makes the Right 'Connections.'" *The Boston Phoenix*, March 23, 1990, sec. 3, pp. 13–14.

New York, The Art Museum Association. *Afro-American Abstraction*. Exhibition catalogue by April Kingsley. New York, 1982.

New York, Germans van Eck Gallery. *After Nature*. Exhibition brochure by Steven Henry Madoff. New York, 1986.

New York, R.C. Erpf Gallery. *Private Works for Public Spaces*. Exhibition brochure by Jenny Dixon. New York, 1988.

New York, The Museum of Modern Art. *An International Survey of Recent Painting and Sculpture*. Exhibition catalogue by Kynaston McShine. New York, 1984.

————. *Primitivism in 20th Century Art: Affinity of the Tribal and the Modern*. Exhibition catalogue by William S. Rubin and Kirk Varnedoe. New York, 1984.

New York, The New Museum of Contemporary Art. *The Decade Show: Frameworks of Identity in the 1980s*. Exhibition catalogue. New York, 1990.

New York, Oscarsson Hood Gallery. *The New Spiritualism: Transcendent Images in Painting and Sculpture*. Exhibition catalogue by April Kingsley. New York, 1981.

New York, The Solomon R. Guggenheim Museum. *Young American Artists, 1978 Exxon National Exhibition*. Exhibition catalogue by Linda Shearer. New York, 1978.

————. *Transformations in Sculpture: Four Decades in American and European Art*. Exhibition catalogue by Diane Waldman. New York, 1985.

————. *Emerging Artists 1978–1986: Selections from the Exxon Series*. Exhibition catalogue by Diane Waldman. New York, 1986.

New York, Whitney Museum of American Art. *The Presence of Nature*. Exhibition brochure by Cindy Schwab. New York, 1978.

————. *1979 Biennial Exhibition*. Exhibition catalogue by John G. Hanhardt, Barbara Haskell, Richard Marshall, Mark Segal, and Patterson Sims. New York, 1979.

————. *1981 Biennial Exhibition*. Exhibition catalogue by John G. Hanhardt, Barbara Haskell, Richard Marshall, and Patterson Sims. New York, 1981.

————. *Vital Signs: Organic Abstraction from the Permanent Collection*. Exhibition catalogue by Lisa Phillips. New York, 1988.

————. *1989 Biennial Exhibition*. Exhibition catalogue by Richard Armstrong, John G. Hanhardt, Richard Marshall, and Lisa Phillips. New York, 1989.

_____. *Art in Place: Fifteen Years of Acquisitions*. Exhibition catalogue by Tom Armstrong and Susan C. Larsen. New York, 1989.

New York, Whitney Museum of American Art at Equitable Center. *Enclosing the Void: Eight Contemporary Sculptors*. Exhibition catalogue by Susan Lubowsky. New York, 1988.

"'*New York Times*' Faz Avaliação da 20a Bienal." *Folha de S. Paulo*, October 24, 1989, p. F3.

"News: Sculptor Puryear Celebrated at Biennial." *The Journal of Art* 2, 3 (December 1989), p. 4.

"Nova Escultura Americana." *Folha de S. Paulo*, October 14, 1989, p. 3.

"*N.Y. Times* Destaca Bienal." *O Estado de S. Paulo*, October 17, 1989, p. 3.

Omaha, Nebraska, Joslyn Art Museum. *I-80 Series: Martin Puryear*. Exhibition catalogue by Holliday T. Day. Omaha, 1980.

Opinear, Randy. "The Puryear Exhibition." *Reader* (San Diego), October 11, 1984, pp. 1, 12.

Pereire, Edmar. "Puryear: Alta Arte e Artesanato, na Mesma Forma." *Jornal da Tarde*, February 28, 1989, p. 20.

Philadelphia, Pennsylvania Academy of Fine Arts. *FFA PFFAP: Form and Function, Proposals for Public Art for Philadelphia*. Exhibition catalogue by Penny Belkin Bach. Philadelphia, 1982.

Pimenta, Angela. "Abre a Bienal dos Empresarios Generosos." *O Estado de S. Paulo*, October 14, 1989, p. 1.

Pimenta, Angela, and Norma Freire. "A Dimensão Lírica No Cotidiano de Puryear." *O Estado de S. Paulo*, October 12, 1989, p. 7.

Pincus, Robert L. "A Transformer of Minimalism." *Los Angeles Times*, November 5, 1984, sec. 6, pp. 1, 6.

Pittsburgh, Carnegie Mellon University, Hewlett Art Gallery. *Martin Puryear: Sculpture and Works on Paper*. Exhibition brochure by Elaine King. Pittsburgh, 1987.

Plagens, Peter. "I Just Dropped in to See What Condition My Condition Was in . . . ." *Artscribe International* 56 (February/March 1986), pp. 23–29.

Princenthal, Nancy. "Intuition's Disciplinarian." *Art in America* 77, 7 (January 1990), pp. 130–37, 181.

Providence, Rhode Island, Brown University, Bell Gallery of List Art Center. *Invitational Exhibition: Laurie Anderson, Farrell Brickhouse, Scott Burton, Denise Green, Wolfgang Laib, Joshua Neustein, Lucio Pozzi, Martin Puryear, Haim Steinbach*. Exhibition catalogue by Roger Mayer. Providence, 1982.

"Puryear Foi Escolhido Por Comite Federal." *Folha de S. Paulo*, February 19, 1989, p. E1.

Raczka, Robert. "Martin Puryear." *LA Weekly*, May 5, 1989, p. 126.

Raymond, David. "Museum of Fine Arts/Boston, Connections: Martin Puryear." *Art New England* 11, 6 (June 1990), p. 30.

Raynor, Vivien. "After Nature." *The New York Times*, February 21, 1986, p. C26.

Richard, Paul. "Martin Puryear at Henri 2." *The Washington Post*, 1973. See Benezra essay, note 29.

_____. "A Shrine of Cedar and Hide." *The Washington Post*, July 30, 1977, pp. B1–2.

_____. "The Sculpture of Longing." *The Washington Post*, March 25, 1988, pp. D1–2.

Rickey, Carrie. "Singular Work, Double Bind, Triple Threat." *The Village Voice* 25, 11 (March 3, 1980), p. 71.

Richmond, Virginia, The Institute of Contemporary Art of the Virginia Museum. *American Abstraction Now*. Exhibition catalogue by Julia Boyd. Richmond, 1982.

Robinson, Walter, and Cathy Lebowitz. "Artworld: Puryear Chosen for São Paulo." *Art in America* 77, 1 (January 1989), p. 180.

Rolim, J. Henrique Fabre. "Rompendo Confrontos." *A Tribuna de Santos*, October 14, 1989, n.pag.

Russell, John. "Abstractions from Afro-America." *The New York Times*, March 14, 1980, sec. 3, p. 19.

Saint Louis, The Saint Louis Art Museum. *New Sculpture/Six Artists*. Exhibition brochure by Michael Edward Shapiro. Saint Louis, 1988.

São Paulo. See Jamaica, New York.

"São Paulo Preview." *Art in America* 77, 7 (July 1989), p. 168.

Saunders, Wade. "Art Inc.: The Whitney's 1979 Biennial." *Art in America* 67, 3 (May/June 1979), pp. 96–99.

Schulze, Franz. "Puryear Works: Elegant Simplicity." *Chicago Sun-Times*, May 18, 1980, Show sec., p. 11.

_____. "115 American Artists Expected at Whitney." *Chicago Sun-Times*, March 8, 1981, p. 24.

_____. "It's All in a Matter of Course with New MCA Gift Wrapping." *Chicago Sun-Times*, May 30, 1982, Show sec., p. 4.

Schwabsky, Barry. "The Obscure Objects of Martin Puryear." *Arts* 62, 3 (November 1987), pp. 58–59.

Seattle, Washington, National Oceanic and Atmospheric Administration, Western Regional Center. *Five Artists at NOAA: A Casebook on Art in Public Places*. Essay by Patricia Fuller. Seattle, 1985.

Shipp, E. R. "Art for Those on the Go in Chicago." *The New York Times*, June 16, 1984, sec. L, p. 9.

Silva, Jaime, and Elke Lopes Muniz. "Bienal: A Maneira Mais Fácil de Ver." *O Estado de S. Paulo*, October 31, 1989, pp. 5–6.

Silverthorne, Jeanne. "Martin Puryear." *Artforum* 23, 4 (December 1984), pp. 82–83.

Simmons, Chuck. "Restriking Atavistic Chords." *Artweek* 13, 42 (December 11, 1982), p. 4.

"Simplicidade Complexa de Puryear." *Jornal de Brasilia*, October 15, 1989, p. 1.

Smith, Roberta. "Around Town." *The Village Voice* 24, 36 (September 4, 1984), p. 85.

Smith, Roberta. "A Primitive Look at the Modern." *The Village Voice* 24, 40 (October 2, 1984), p. 85.

Spector, Buzz. "Martin Puryear." *New Art Examiner* 7, 7 (April 1980), p. 22.

Stapen, Nancy. "Making 'Connections' with Works of the Past." *Boston Herald*, April 1, 1990, p. 385.

Stern, William F. "Sculpture Inside Outside." *Cite*, Spring/Summer 1989, pp. 20–21.

Strecker, Marion. "Martin Puryear, Representante dos EUA Na Bienal, Visita Galeria de Arte em São Paulo." *Folha de S. Paulo*, February 28, 1989, p. E3.

———. "Mostra é a Unica Janela Para o Mundo." *Folha de S. Paulo*, February 19, 1989, p. E1.

"Suit Attacks Grant Rules for National Endowment." *The New York Times*, May 24, 1990, p. 132.

Swift, Barbara, and Rob Wilkinson. "The NOAA Program: Public Art on a Shoreline Site." *Landscape Architecture*, September/October 1988, pp. 98–100, 102–03.

Swift, Mary. "Martin Puryear — Protetch/McIntosh Gallery." *The Washington Review* 5, 5 (February/March 1980), p. 21.

Swift, Mary, and Clarissa Wittenberg. "An Interview with Martin Puryear." *The Washington Review* 4, 3 (October/November 1978), p. 33.

Tannous, David. "Martin Puryear at the Corcoran." *Art in America* 66, 3 (May/June 1978), pp. 119–20.

———. "Those Who Stay." *Art in America* 66, 4 (July/August 1978), p. 85.

Tavares, Carlos. "A Madeira Viva de Martin Puryear na Bienal de SP." *Correio Braziliense*, October 11, 1989, p. 7.

Taylor, Robert. "Sculpture Show a Pioneering Effort." *The Boston Globe*, May 18, 1986, pp. A17, 20.

Taylor, Sue. "Poetic Resonance Marks Puryear's New Sculpture." *Chicago Sun-Times*, October 23, 1985, p. 50.

———. "Report from Minneapolis: Garden City." *Art in America* 76, 12 (December 1988), pp. 28–36.

Teltsch, Kathleen. "MacArthur Foundation Honors Achievement." *The New York Times*, July 18, 1989, p. A18.

Temin, Christine. "Puryear's Primitive Sophistication." *The Boston Globe*, July 7, 1984, p. 8.

———. "The Time of Martin Puryear." *The Boston Globe*, March 25, 1990, pp. 25, 28–29.

Thalenberg, Eileen. "Site Work: Some Sculpture at Artpark." *Artscanada* 216/217 (October/November 1977), pp. 16–20.

Thorson, Alice. "Separate but More Than Equal." *The Washington Times*, January 29, 1987, p. B3.

Tomkins, Calvin, "Perception at All Levels." *The New Yorker* 60, 42 (December 3, 1984), pp. 176–81.

Trebay, Guy. "Museum Pieces." *The Village Voice* 30, 8 (February 19, 1985), p. 75.

Tully, Judd. "On Custom and Culture." *Skyline* (Chicago), Summer 1979, p. 11.

———. "Chicago Art Scene." *Flash Art* 103 (Summer 1981), p. 26.

"20a Bienal e Aberta Sem Estar Pronta; Somem Duas Obras de Dale Chihuly." *Folha de S. Paulo*, October 15, 1989, p. D1.

"23 Mil Metros Quadrad." *Folha de S. Paulo*, October 14, 1989, p. 4.

University Park, Illinois, Governors State University. *The Nathan Manilow Sculpture Park.* Essay by Peter Schjeldahl. University Park, 1987.

University Park, Pennsylvania, The Pennsylvania State University Museum of Art. *The Material Dominant: Some Current Artists and Their Media.* Exhibition brochure. University Park, 1977.

Varro, Barbara. "Olympic Art." *Chicago Sun-Times*, August 14, 1983, Living sec., p. 2.

Warren, Lynne, and Jeffrey Edelstein. "Artworld Chicago 1981." *Images and Issues* 2, 3 (Winter 1981–82), pp. 44–47.

Washington, D.C., The Corcoran Gallery of Art. *Edelson, Puryear, Scanga, Stackhouse.* Exhibition brochure by Christopher French. Washington, D.C., 1988.

Weiss, Heidi. "City Sculpture." *New Art Examiner* 9, 1 (October 1981), p. 18.

Westerbeck, Colin. "Chicago: Martin Puryear, Chicago Public Library Cultural Center." *Artforum* 25 (May 1987), p. 154.

Wingert, Pat. "Arty Stops in Store for Trains to O'Hare." *Chicago Sun-Times*, July 17, 1983, Chicago Area sec., p. 23.

Wittenburg, Clarissa K. "Martin Puryear." *Art Voices; South* 2, 1 (January/February 1979), p. 19.

Wright, Martha McWilliams. "Washington Letter." *Art International* 21, 5 (October/November 1978), pp. 64–65.

Zimmer, William. "Art for the Me Decade." *The Soho Weekly News*, March 1, 1979, p. 39.